W9-DGH-226

The Master Builders

LIBRARY OF MEDIEVAL CIVILIZATION
EDITED BY JOAN EVANS AND
PROFESSOR CHRISTOPHER BROOKE

JOHN HARVEY

The Master Builders
ARCHITECTURE
IN THE MIDDLE AGES

McGRAW-HILL BOOK COMPANY · NEW YORK

Contents

General Editor's Preface

In 1966 a large and handsome book was published by Messrs Thames and Hudson, with the title *The Flowering of the Middle Ages*. The text was provided by a team of scholars under the shrewd and skilful captaincy of Joan Evans, and could be read with pleasure and profit by all those who could afford to buy the book, and had an ample lectern on which to lay it. Word has come to the publishers that there are many who have smaller pockets and less ambitious furniture, who would like none the less to read its chapters as well as to admire the *Flowering*'s illustrations. They therefore asked me to join with Dr Evans in the pleasant task of converting the book into a series of small volumes, each incorporating a chapter of the original. The old chapters have been roused, stretched and shaken into a new and somewhat enlarged shape, have donned their old costume of pictures considerably increased, and now present themselves to the public for inspection. Their enlargement is designed to make them more self-contained, able to walk the world on their own; yet they remain a series none the less, and hope still to walk often in company with one another.

It is with great pleasure that I present to the public my colleagues' books in the Series. As I do so, I recall many kindnesses from many members of Thames and Hudson, and especially from the late Walter Neurath, who inspired the *Flowering*. I give thanks too, and above all, to Joan Evans, who first enlisted me in *Flowering* and has so readily welcomed and supported my collaboration in this revival and revision.

CHRISTOPHER BROOKE

6

Foreword
to the Original Edition

Fifty years ago history was mainly studied in school and university, and as a consequence by the educated reader, in terms of wars, political alliances and constitutional developments. Its base was properly in written documents, and even social history was not envisaged in other than documentary terms. Eight half-tone illustrations were enough for any historical work and most were not illustrated at all.

Now, at least for the general reader, all is changed. Schoolmasters attempt to give some visual background to their history lessons; occasionally even a professor of history may show a few slides. Professional historians and archivists rightly continue to study every facet of their subject in documented detail, but for most people 'history' has become a much more general matter, that provides them with a background to what they see and what they read. For them, at least, historians must so interpret the documents as to make them reveal the life of the past rather than its battles and its political machinations.

This change is due less to the professional historians themselves than to a change of view in the reading public: a change that can only be paralleled in the second half of the nineteenth century when trains and steamers made it easy to travel and everyone began to know their Europe. That time produced its Ruskin and its Viollet-le-Duc, its Lasteyrie and its Henry Adams; but we forget that Ruskin had to draw, or to engage others to draw for him, the things he wrote and talked about, and that Viollet-le-Duc was never able to reproduce a photograph.

In our own day a new wave of travel by car and plane has been accompanied by incredible developments in photography and in reproduction. Black and white photographs and half-tone blocks revolutionized the study of architecture and art at the end of the nineteenth century, and the great archaeological discoveries of the day made the general public willing to accept an object or a building *pari passu* with a written document. In our own time colour photographs and colour plates have enriched these studies in a way that would have seemed miraculous to Ruskin.

Moreover, though education remains astonishingly bookish, our recreations have trained our eyes. An experienced and successful lecturer of 1900 said that a slide must remain on the screen for at least a minute to give the audience time to take it in. Now, the cinema screen and the television set have trained us in visual nimbleness, and we 'see' much more quickly. . . .

Somewhere about 1100 it seems as if Europe settled on an even keel. In England the Norman dynasty had established itself militarily and administratively. In France Philip I had established a rival kingdom, the Cluniac reform had revivified religious life, and the Crusades had started on their way. In Germany Henry IV was establishing the Empire on a firmer basis. In Italy Pope Gregory VII had lost his fight against the Emperor, but had gained new spiritual force for Rome. In Spain Alfonso VI of Castile had made Toledo the capital of Christian Spain, and the Cid had conquered Valencia. In the Eastern Empire the Comneni had suffered the inroads first of the Normans and then of the Crusaders; the weight of power was shifting westward. In Europe it is fair to say that a measure of stability had been achieved, in which the forces of feudalism, monasticism, scholastic philosophy and civic growth could work together to make the history of the Middle Ages.

To make that history more real to the ordinary reader is our purpose. The authors have not here published unknown documents, unknown monuments or unknown works of art, but have tried by the interpretation of what is known to make the Christian civilization of Europe in the Middle Ages more significant and more comprehensible to the readers of today. The keyword to our conception of history is civilization.

JOAN EVANS

8

Chapter One

The Mason's Skill

The Middle Ages exert a fascination over the modern mind largely because of their art which, in spite of tragic losses, survives in massive quantity. Like all art, that produced in Europe between the fall of Rome and the coming of the Renaissance is the concrete expression of an outlook which informed society. Art comprises the whole of man's works, the material outcome of his thought as expressed by his hands and through the tools of his invention. Within this total orbit art may be subdivided according to the senses to which it appeals, as poetry and music do to the ear; or classified in a hierarchy of purpose wherein the arts of merely practical concern rank below the fine arts regarded as an inessential luxury appealing to a faculty of highly educated appreciation. This latter distinction not only overlooks the essential character of fine art, but also obscures the fundamental unity of the skills involved in artistic production. While an artefact may have positive utility wholly divorced from aesthetic quality, the converse does not hold good: all true art, aesthetically speaking, rests upon a sound grasp of underlying craftmanship. It is due to the close identification between efficient craftsmanship and aesthetic perception during the Middle Ages that the art of the period has so intense an interest.

Discussion of an artistic culture requires that its origins must be fixed in place and time. Here we are concerned primarily with western Europe from Iceland and Ireland to Poland and Hungary, from Norway to Portugal and Italy: in fact the sum total of those lands whose religion was Western Christianity owing allegiance to Rome. In time, the age as a whole intervened between the collapse of the western Roman Empire in the fifth century and the deliberate re-creation in the fifteenth of neo-Roman arts and techniques based upon surviving written texts and upon study of architectural and technical remains. Within this total period of a thousand years we must here discuss the second five hundred, for between the

9

fifth century and the tenth stretched the Dark Ages of retrogression and resurgent savagery. In spite of their barbarism these early centuries were mysteriously shot through with glimpses of highly imaginative art and were alive with aspirations towards a future level of achievement.

Beside the continuity of Byzantine art, the unending miracle of Chinese sensitivity and poise, or the precocious brilliance of Islam, all possessing long and augmented traditions of science and techniques, the contribution of north-western Europe between the years 400 and 900 must seem provincial at best. Admirable as may be individual works, some of them noble and even awe-inspiring relics of an age of simplicity, it would be vain to seek among the Franks, Goths, Anglo-Saxons and Scandinavians for any capacity for organization on the grand scale. The greatest cathedrals, monasteries or palaces are insignificant when compared with the ruins left by the Romans or even the earliest of the magnificent buildings of the resurgent eleventh century. Whether or no we attach major historical significance to the millennial hypothesis – that men who believed in the end of the world at AD 1000 would devote scant attention to grandiose material projects – it is a fact that it was the eleventh century that witnessed a profound change in outlook. Hitherto a collection of small units thinking of local affairs, Europe was suddenly transformed. Tiny principalities gave way before the concept of nationality and political unification took the place of empty theories such as that of the Bretwalda (or sovereign of Britain). The geographical insularity of Britain may in this way have been responsible for the emergence of the nation-state elsewhere. What is certain is that by the eleventh century notions of co-ordination, not only political but also economic and technical, were current and were beginning to give rise to the possibility of grand constructions emulating one another and leading to ever greater and more noble scale.

The question of scale is of the utmost importance since mere size involves a high degree of constructional organization. Even the largest buildings of Carolingian times, such as the palace and chapel of Charlemagne at Aachen (792–805), had roofs of relatively small span. No outstanding competence in the designing of centring or scaffolding was called for; the details of architectural design were either closely copied from Roman or Byzantine work or

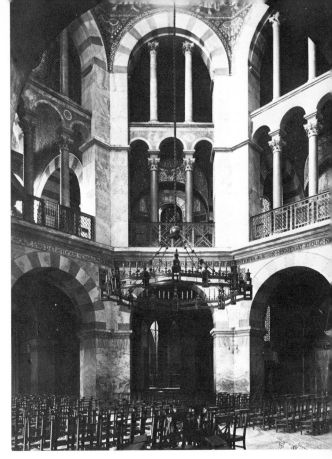

1 Charlemagne's palace chapel at Aachen, built between 792 and 805, was among the most ambitious buildings of its age. But in comparison with a Romanesque church of 200 years later its scale is extremely modest

were extremely crude. The beginning of a new competence in design on a much larger scale can be seen from the very start of the eleventh century. In churches this appears in Saint-Martin at Tours (*c.* 1000–50), Saint-Bénigne at Dijon (1001–18) and in the other grandiose churches built through the century and culminating in Santiago de Compostela begun about 1075, and the new church of the monastery of Cluny started 1088 and finished in 1121. In secular buildings the capacity to build on a notable scale is shown by the Imperial Hall at Goslar (*c.* 1040–50) measuring internally some 145 feet by 45 and, to a far greater degree, by the great hall of William Rufus at Westminster, built in 1097–99 and measuring 238 by 68 feet, the largest room in Europe for well over a century. It will bear comparison even with the central hall of the Basilica of Constantine at Rome (AD 312), which measured some 265 by 82 feet.

97

A revolution was in progress, or rather a series of revolutions. The first stage is marked by the desire to build on a large scale, even if crudely, and most of the constructional experts involved seem to have come from Italy. In the case of Saint-Bénigne at Dijon we actually know that the work was directed by the Italian William of Volpiano (near Turin in Piedmont), who brought Italian masters. The second stage, far more concerned with niceties of design and capable of even larger buildings, occupied the second half of the century. About the year 1100 this second stage was itself overtaken by a third wave of still greater accomplishment. The achievements of the later Middle Ages are due to the new skills brought by the leaders of this threefold revolution of the eleventh century.

Who then were the leaders of this serial revolution? The precise answer in terms of human individuals may remain for ever unknown, but in a general sense it may be said that they were masons. To most modern readers this will suggest a group of artisans in a yard or shed, hacking away at blocks of stone with mallet and cold-chisel, to the accompaniment possibly of a stone-saw slicing free-stone and powered by a sputtering oil-engine and certainly over-laid with a fine layer of dust. It has to be explained that this picture differs widely from the historical truth regarding those masons who were responsible for the design of ever larger and more complex buildings in the years 1000–1300.

Not only has the English word 'mason' somewhat changed its meaning in the course of centuries of usage; its derivation is a mystery, and it is consequently impossible to state clearly what its original sense was. By the period with which we are here concerned the various forms of the word had become confused with the Old French *maisoner*, to build (i.e. make a house), and the mason was any builder, but more particularly *the* builder who had direction of works and who was responsible for their design: what we now think of as an architect. Although the word came later to be used in contradistinction to *carpenter*, a builder in timber, a mason might have expert knowledge of both stone- and wood-working, and throughout the Middle Ages there were survivals of this overall competence, in spite of the tendency of the later craft-guilds to insist upon a specialized delimitation of jobs.

In modern times, especially in England, there has been a sharp antithesis between the designer of buildings, known as an architect, and their constructor, called generically a builder, and comprising a number of separate crafts, notably those of mason (dealing with stonework), carpenter (working in wood), tiler, plumber, plasterer, painter – with the bricklayer as a specialized type of mason concerned with the use of the standardized synthetic stones formed of burned clay by analogy with roof-tiles. The mediaeval sense of mason is far less specific and could be general and almost all-inclusive, and it comprehended both the master who designed and gave the orders, and the skilled artisan who carried them into effect. We must, therefore, understand 'mason' in the same way that we think of 'musician', as comprising the composer, the conductor and the members of the orchestra.

Little is known as to the educational methods adopted by the masons of periods earlier than the thirteenth century. It can be deduced from the successive styles of work produced that during the three hundred years after AD 1000 there must have been several marked improvements both in the techniques employed by the craftsmen and in the knowledge available to the masters responsible for the design of buildings. It is reasonably certain that, before the appearance in the thirteenth century of the legal system of formal apprenticeship of pupils to a master, training was in practice from father to son, or at any rate from an elder to a younger member of the same family. Craft skills ran in families and were in fact quite often the stock-in-trade of a tribe: hence the element of secrecy which accounts not only for much of the mystery regarding mediaeval architecture, but also in part for the disappearance of most technical drawings used.

What little we know of the masons of the later Dark Ages suggests that they came from Rome and from northern Italy, where there was in the seventh and eighth centuries a recognized organization of building masters under the Lombard kings. This was probably to some extent a survival of the guilds (*collegia*) of Roman times, and it is all but certain that it was this organization that provided the framework for the later congregations of masons in the various regions of mediaeval Europe. The name given to these masters, '*comacini*', has nothing to do with the lake or city of Como, as used to be thought, but simply means 'associated masons'.

Contrary also to the fantastic web of wild suppositions built upon only two specific references in laws of 643, these masters did not travel in groups producing all the major buildings of Europe: like architects of all periods, they normally took charge singly, or collaborated in quite small partnerships. It is probable, all the same, that groups of working masons as well as one or more masters had to be induced to travel from Italy to the remoter areas, as when St Wilfrid had his buildings at Hexham built by craftsmen from Rome. Not until a fair proficiency on the part of the working masons had been attained within a given region was it possible to dispense with the aid of foreigners.

Although there are a few indications of moderate competence in building, in Britain and in other parts of north-western Europe, by the end of the Dark Ages, there was, as we have seen, very little work on a substantial scale until after AD 1000. It is probably no coincidence that the eleventh-century developments which are associated with the rise of the fully Romanesque style were contemporary with the first of a series of waves of political action in which the West undertook a counter-campaign against the Muslims, both in Spain and in the Holy Land. This campaign included several crusades within the two or three generations before the so-called First Crusade preached in 1095. Even hostile contacts with the East, that is to say with the world of Islam, were productive of noteworthy results. As we shall see, successful forays resulted in the capture of Saracens, many of whom were artists and craftsmen; but even apart from this, the penetration of the South by relatively barbarous northerners such as the Normans, provided a glimpse of the comforts of higher civilization. There was a direct incentive to emulate such relative luxury in the northern homeland, and in spite of the climatic difficulties a successful transfer was accomplished.

The driving force behind this whole movement was external in origin: it depended upon the human types of greater refinement who dwelt around the Mediterranean area and who, generation after generation, influenced the northern kings and nobles by repeated intermarriages. The greater sophistication which resulted made ever more adroit use of the available resources, notably the highly energetic manpower of the Normans in their expansive mood of the eleventh century. The barbarous crudity of most of the Western crusaders was what impressed their opponents, who

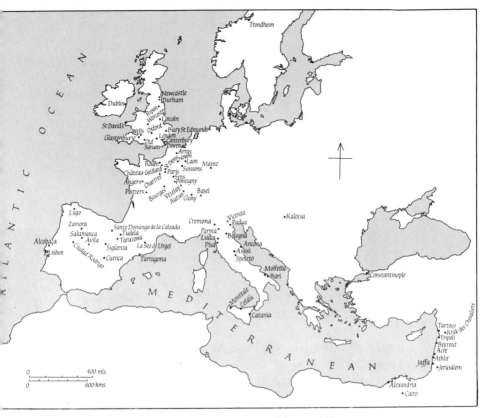

The following place names appear on the map:

Trondheim

ATLANTIC OCEAN

Dublin · Newcastle · Durham · Ripon · Worcester · Lincoln · St David's · Wells · Oxford · Bury St Edmunds · Glastonbury · Old Sarum · London · Canterbury · Dover · Arras · Noyon · Rouen · St Denis · Laon · Mainz · Château-Gaillard · Paris · Soissons · Angers · Chartres · Sens · Pontigny · Poitiers · Bourges · Vézelay · Autun · Cluny · Basel

Lugo · Zamora · Salamanca · Avila · Alcobaça · Lisbon · Ciudad Rodrigo · Santo Domingo de la Calzada · Tudela · Tarazona · Sigüenza · La Seo de Urgel · Cuenca · Tarragona

Cremona · Vicenza · Padua · Parma · Lucca · Bologna · Pisa · Ancona · Assisi · Spoleto · Molfetta · Bari · Monreale · Cefalù · Catania

Kalocsa

Constantinople

MEDITERRANEAN

Tartous · Krak des Chevaliers · Tripoli · Beyrout · Acre · Athlit · Jaffa · Jerusalem · Alexandria · Cairo

0   400 mls.
0   600 kms.

2 Sites of the chief architectural monuments of the twelfth century

nevertheless realized the threat they represented. It is, strangely enough, a tribute to the basic character of the Franks that in the long run they were able to retire from the Near East, defeated on the field of battle yet in the course of two centuries improved almost out of recognition. The western Europe through which Edward I returned to England in 1274 was far removed from the tumultuous chaos in which Norman bands had carved out kingdoms only two hundred years earlier. Even the leaders of those Norman raids had shown an amazing capacity for organization, and it was precisely this that made possible the rise of Western civilization. More to our immediate purpose, it was the essential prerequisite for the production of complex buildings on a large scale.

15

Not merely the sophisticated demand for refined surroundings had infiltrated the West: a great deal of the capacity to fulfil that demand also came from outside the area of north-western Europe with which we are concerned. To a much slighter extent this had been prefigured at an earlier stage of development. Even in the Dark Ages there had been occasional glimpses of higher aesthetic quality or technical capacity, usually to be connected with the arrival in some Western country of clerics or artists from the Near East, and both Syrian and Armenian influences have been traced in Visigothic, British and Irish art. In the earlier period, however, the number of such contacts was slight and their effects minimal. The events of the eleventh century show that much more direct contacts, affecting considerable numbers of persons, must have been involved. Consideration of historical and geographical factors suggests several main lines of influence.

So far as concerns Britain there is little evidence for the onset of major building in the early part of the eleventh century, but the rebuilding of devastated churches and monasteries under Canute, the son of a Polish princess, may reflect some Byzantine influences brought by the overland route. Rather more direct contacts between northern Europe and the civilized lands of the Mediterranean followed the conquest of southern Italy and Sicily by the Normans in the generation after 1042. Perhaps even more fruitful, as a source of skilled craftsmen, was the siege and capture of Barbastro in the north-east of Spain in 1064. An army of Normans and Frenchmen, with the blessing of the Pope and under the command of William VIII, Duke of Aquitaine, took many Moorish prisoners, sending several thousand into France, 1,500 to Rome and 7,000 to Constantinople. Singers, musicians and other artists are stated to have been among the number, and presumably also the Moorish corps of engineers which had defended Barbastro. It seems probable that the spoils of war included a substantial number of craftsmen who possessed a degree of technical skill hitherto unknown north of the Alps and Pyrenees.

Such contacts between Normans and Saracens go far towards explaining the ambitious architectural programme which became manifest in northern France and in England shortly before, and in the generation succeeding, the Norman Conquest of 1066. Fully developed Romanesque (in England, Norman) architecture

16

3 The new cathedral of St Swithun at Winchester, begun in 1079

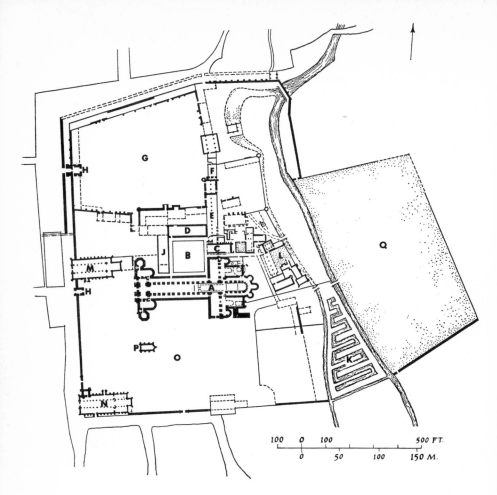

100   0   100   500 FT.

0   50   100   150 M.

includes much work of small scale: the little village churches and the rare stone houses of merchants or Jews. The very large number of such small buildings, however, implies a considerable force of skilled men, while the relatively few buildings on a grand scale must have tested to the utmost the capacity for organization available in that age.

     The Palatine abbey of Durham (1093–1140), the new cathedral *3* and priory of St Swithun at Winchester (1079–1120), and above all *4, 5* such a gigantic church and monastery as that of Bury St Edmunds (1081–*c.* 1130), well exemplify the new ability to think and to build big. The royal and noble patrons and distinguished clerics shared

4, 5 The Benedictine
abbey of Bury St Edmunds
– the plan and (*right*) the
Norman gatehouse. A,
abbey church; B, cloister;
C, chapter-house;
D, refectory;
E, dormitory; F, abbot's
palace; G, great court;
H, the two gate-houses;
J, great hall; K, fish-pond;
L, infirmary; M, church
of St James; N, church of
St Mary; O, cemetery;
P, charnel house;
Q, vineyard

with the master masons who worked for them this capacity to en-
visage grandiose concepts; and it was the masons who developed
the practical organization and techniques involved in their realiza-
tion. With few exceptions the great Romanesque buildings erected
in England were larger than their counterparts in France or elsewhere on the continent of Europe. This was probably due to the
'colonial' aspect of Norman power in England. Whereas France
was already well supplied with churches and monasteries, England
came as a virgin field for architectural expansion and experiment.
Even the greatest of the Saxon minsters were small, and the colleges
of priests or abbeys of unreformed Benedictines must have seemed

19

fit only for demolition and total replacement. The extent of the resulting campaign of reconstruction in early Norman England placed the country in the forefront of an architectural revolution comparable in character only to the Industrial Revolution eight centuries later.

Labour and transport

The political unification of England under the Norman kings and the subordination of the feudal system in England to the power of the Crown made it possible to raise large funds for building. Yet even assured finances could not of themselves have enabled a visionary programme to become effective. The masters responsible had to be able, not merely to plan and design suitable buildings, structurally stable and aesthetically pleasing to their clients, but also to organize the provision of great gangs of men and the acquisition and transport of vast quantities of materials. The extent to which Caen stone, already quarried on a large scale in Normandy and within easy reach of water carriage, was imported for use in England is one of the factors which indicate the dependence of the early generations of our Romanesque builders upon headquarters overseas.

During the late eleventh century, in England and on the Continent, the difficulty of attracting a sufficient number of skilled craftsmen to a building site, possibly remote, must have been very great. It is not at all clear, in fact, how the greater jobs were manned. Later in the Middle Ages the royal power of impressment was freely used, not only by the Crown, but by other building owners who paid for licences to make use of this prerogative. It is known that by the thirteenth or fourteenth century it was normal for men to be recruited even from very distant parts of the country. In 1233 carpenters taken at Reading were sent to Painscastle in Radnorshire, about 120 miles off, and were allowed journey money of 1s. 4d. each. Certainly there must, even in earlier times, have been ways and means of encouraging, or even forcing, men possessed of the needed skills to converge upon the major sites.

Transport of materials made great demands, not only on the funds available, but also upon the logistic ability of the masters. All communications were slow, and every stage of the operations had in consequence to be worked out well in advance. Yet we find,

20

not only that very large amounts of stone were imported from Caen, but that stone at many quarries was worked to shape before transport, on a basis of patterns drawn on parchment or canvas and sent in advance. Since land transport was excessively costly, much ingenuity was expended in working out feasible routes for water carriage. The stone for Bury, some of it from Caen and some from Barnack in Northamptonshire, was taken by boat to points within about ten miles of the abbey, by the sea and up the Gipping in one case, and through Fenland waterways to the Little Ouse in the other. When Abingdon Abbey was rebuilt soon after 1100, the great timbers for roof-beams and rafters were brought from Shrewsbury in six wains drawn by twelve oxen each, and the journey is recorded as having taken six or seven weeks coming and going. Since the return journey is about 220 miles, this implies a rate of progress of only five miles a day, a clear indication of the state of the roads. That such journeys were not merely possible, but must have been frequent, shows the ingenuity and determination of the men who organized them.

The earlier Norman masons were not yet fully competent to design the large structures which they were attempting. A considerable number of their great towers fell down and, in spite of some attempts to attribute such catastrophes to divine vengeance or satanic interference, there were contemporary chroniclers shrewd enough to suspect inadequacy of craftmanship or poor foundations. It must, also, be remembered that for a generation or more after the Conquest the English labour force was largely composed of Saxons unused to large-scale operations. Their employment produced in many instances the phenomenon of the 'Saxon overlap', when buildings obviously erected under Norman auspices show Saxon characteristics in detail. It was not to be expected that with such a mixed force of men, with very few masters of really outstanding ability, the vast campaign of works should be carried out without some collapsing. It was only as time went on that the burning of lime was perfected to produce adequate mortar, and the roughly shaped small stones of early work gave place to exquisitely true blocks of ashlar.

The production of finely worked ashlar was one of the key 'inventions' (really an importation) that made possible the final developments of Romanesque architecture, and later the rise of a new aesthetic style now known to us as Gothic. Before passing on to a consideration of Gothic architecture as the mature fruit of mediaeval culture we must give some retrospective thought to the phenomenon of Romanesque. It has been fashionable in recent years to restrict this term to quite late developments of the eleventh and twelfth centuries, but this has been to lose sight of the fact that for a hundred years or more the word 'Romanesque' has come to have a perfectly clear general usage. According to this usage the sense includes the whole of those styles of building 'prevalent in Romanized Europe between the classical and the Gothic periods'. The abandonment of terms already fully a part of the language can result only in confusion, and Romanesque in the full sense should be understood to comprehend all architecture based in any way upon Roman precedents, and extending from roughly AD 400 to the onset of Gothic in the twelfth century. It is permissible to distinguish many phases and different regional or social styles within this long epoch of some 750 years, but it would be out of place to do so here.

What all these Romanesque styles have in common, as opposed to their classical precedent and their Gothic successor, is that they were produced by craftsmen with seriously defective technical resources. The sophisticated skills of the building crafts that had been described by Vitruvius in the Augustan Age were very largely destroyed by the barbarian invasions. It was not merely that different (and cruder) patrons called for a less sophisticated style or a rougher finish; the capacity to produce even a fully competent copy of earlier work no longer existed. This leads to a further point: that mere copying of any past style, for the sake of its surface effect, is an artistic confession of failure and leads to decay. It is only a living art in constant change due to repeated fresh experiment that has the power to overcome and, in the long run, to survive. Hence the production of architecture within western Europe in the centuries of the Dark Ages has hardly any structural or aesthetic value, however great its archaeological interest. To this extent it is understandable that Romanesque as an active style worthy of the name should be felt to belong only to the later centuries in which flourished the Carolingian, Ottonian, Lombardic and Burgundo-Norman styles of architecture and of art.

Even in this later period the technical inadequacy of the builders is painfully obvious. Construction is excessively massive, because there was little or no experimental knowledge of stability, and it is important to realize that this uneconomical waste continued even through the very late phases of Romanesque. It was not until the advent of the first Gothic that the precisely jointed ashlar masonry, largely eliminating the mass of rubble core, made possible thin walls and slender shafts. Progressive attenuation of structure, though it had started in the eleventh century, only reached a significant stage during the twelfth. It is indeed this attenuation that provides a quantitative index to the real advances made. Architectural design is an art, whose success can only be judged subjectively according to taste and opinion yet its structural expression, necessarily related to the operation of natural laws, is scientific and subject to an objective and factual analysis. Judged by this scientific (even if experimental rather than theoretical) approach, Western architecture was improving slowly in the first half of the eleventh century, more rapidly after 1050, and swept upwards to supreme success in the two centuries that followed 1100.

We can only guess at the specific causes of the first slow change, moving away from the inertia of the Dark Ages. It is certain that some part was played by the arrival in the West of Byzantine artists exiled from Constantinople and the Empire by the onset of the iconoclastic movement. This movement lasted for well over a hundred years, from early in the eighth century to the middle of the ninth, and caused large colonies of Greek religious and Greek artists to move into southern Italy and single individuals to scatter further afield. Byzantine links with Venice were also responsible for a seepage of artistic and technical information from Byzantium to the Lombardic zone. In course of time this led to some degree of revivification of old skills. Architectural details and sculpture began to show more refinement, but it is evident that the grave risks inherent in large-scale structural experimentation prevented the production of buildings of more than moderate size. What little we know of the architects of the time suggests that they were aware of their own deficiencies: they were commonly brought together as committees or discussion-groups, to reach solutions to technical problems out of their pooled knowledge. This contrasts sharply with the Gothic norm of the single master, which was already supplanting the earlier system in Norman times, as for

23

6, 7 example at St Albans Abbey (1077–88, continuing to 1115), where the master, Robert, achieved outstanding fame.

Besides the change from massive rubble walls to thinner but stronger works of ashlar, and that from uncertain craftsmen seeking mutual advice to self-confident architects dictating to the workmen, there must have been another transformation which we can deduce from examination of the structures. In the earlier period the stones used had been small and such as could be carried singly 8, 13 by hand. Clearly such hoisting machinery as existed was very simple and incapable of raising heavy weights. In England it is possible to narrow down to within a few years of 1100 the date of introduction of improved plant. This date is highly suggestive of the direct importation of Saracen machinery brought back by returning Crusaders from their victorious campaign. As we shall shortly see, Saracen prisoners are likely to have played a leading part in the next stage of stylistic development, and it is reasonable to include mechanical devices, too, as part of the booty.

6, 7, 8 St Albans Abbey, in course of construction at the end of the eleventh and beginning of the twelfth centuries, under Master Robert. *Above:* the crossing tower. *Left:* view of the interior of the nave from the crossing. *Right:* work in progress, from a manuscript of the thirteenth century

9 The vault of Durham Cathedral (originally
1104), probably the first high rib-vault
in Europe

Chapter Two

Gothic Origins

It was then in the opening years of the twelfth century that the onset of the late Norman period was characterized by a new ability to produce really fine worked ashlar; by the use of larger stones implying better cranes and hoists; and by the evident self-reliance of individual masters. The first of these factors was sufficiently obvious to leave its mark on recorded history: mortar joints had become so fine that a chronicler commented on Bishop Roger's buildings at Old Sarum, begun soon after 1102, that the stones were so accurately set that the whole work might be thought cut out of a single rock. At Winchester, where the first Norman tower had fallen in 1107, the rebuilding contrasts markedly with *10* the original build of only twenty to thirty years before. Although England happens to provide this excellent evidence for the date of change, the new style of work can be seen throughout western Europe. This sudden revolution in technique bears all the marks of external impact, and could not have been the result of a slow evolution in traditional skills. There can be no mere coincidence in the fact that exactly such skill had existed among the stonemasons of the Near East for centuries, and that at this very date the great campaign known (inaccurately) as the First Crusade had just taken place.

We have already seen that earlier crusades had been in progress more than a generation before, and had achieved some important successes such as the capture of Barbastro. The Norman conquest of Sicily from the Arabs provides another example of the same phenomenon, and within a generation of the Battle of Hastings the whole of the West was beginning to benefit from the contacts established with centres of older and higher culture. The details may be hard to establish, but the main fact is evident. Greater precision is possible over the First Crusade. It was launched by Pope Urban II with an appeal on 27 November 1095. Large bodies of

troops were gathered and converged upon Constantinople a year later. During the summer of 1097 Nicaea was taken and the Seljuk Turks defeated in Anatolia; in 1098 Antioch was captured and a 'western' principality founded, still further to the east, at Edessa (now Urfa). The Crusade was crowned with success when Jerusalem fell, after a six weeks' siege, on 15 July 1099.

The new Eastern dominions of the Franks, as the Western crusaders were called, were defended by an extensive chain of castles which called forth the fullest resources of the military engineers and masons. There is no doubt that many developments in fortification took place as a result of the experience gained on the Crusades and especially through the opportunities for examining Byzantine, Armenian and Saracenic defences and interrogating local craftsmen. It may be supposed that returning Frankish engineers from 1099 onwards would have come back equipped with fresh knowledge of structural expedients, and that a propor-tion of Eastern prisoners of outstanding capacity were brought back to the West. At least one such prisoner, 'Lalys', built Neath Abbey and is said to have been architect to Henry I. Nor did the matter end there, for it is only from Eastern sources that the Western architects can have acquired the pointed arch which was to become the symbol and chief mark of the Gothic style. To this extent it must be accepted that Sir Christopher Wren was right in supposing, some three centuries ago, that the origins of the Gothic style were to be found in the Eastern buildings seen by the crusaders. Whether or no the invention of the ribbed cross-vault is likewise Eastern (and vault-ribs of a relevant kind were certainly built in
9   Persia and in Armenia before 1100), it is at Durham Cathedral that

it was first seen in the West, so far as exhaustive investigations can show. The first stone of the church at Durham was laid on 11 August 1093, and the wooden centring of the vaults is known to have been removed only just in time for the translation of the body of St Cuthbert on 4 September 1104. It is a very strange coincidence, if indeed it be a coincidence at all, that the first known ribbed vault in the West should have been built within the five years that succeeded the taking of Jerusalem.

The precise date at which the Eastern pointed arch is first evidenced in western Europe is a matter of controversy. It is generally accepted as an original feature of the arcades of the great church of Cluny, begun in 1088 and finished as far as the transepts by 1100. Professor Kenneth J. Conant regards the source of these arches as the Benedictine monastery church of Monte Cassino, rebuilt in 1066–71, by craftsmen some of whom were from Amalfi, a commercial republic with trading stations in the Near East and as far away as Baghdad. What is quite certain is that such pointed arches, on a grand scale, formed part of the design of Autun *11* Cathedral, built in 1120–32, and that they were linked with the cross-rib vault in the narthex of the abbey of Saint-Denis, built for *12* Abbot Suger before 1140. From then onwards Gothic style existed.

11, 12 Pointed arches, at Autun (*left*), 1120–32, and Saint-Denis (*above*), before 1140

29

13 Thirteenth-century masons. Stones, shaped by the two men bottom right, are lifted by a hoisting engine powered by the tread-wheel on the left. Another man is carrying mortar up the ladder on his back

Dimension and design

Apart from the technical skill to cut stone to true shapes, to lay foundations, to work out adequate scaffolding and temporary supports for arches, vaults and roofs, the building masters must certainly have acquired a knowledge of principles of design. It is evident, partly from study of the buildings, partly from treatises written later, that this knowledge consisted quite largely in systems of proportion. The pupil architect was taught, by his father, uncle or master, certain methods of geometrical setting-out, and certain geometrical and numerical formulae. Basic to the problems of the mediaeval mason was the setting-out of a correct right angle upon the ground; and, as few laymen would then have known, the simplest method of doing this was and is to lay down, with pegs and cord, a triangle with sides measured as 3, 4 and 5. The knowledge of a number of such problems in practical geometry, series of numbers and methods of subdivision, would provide the architect with the essentials of his skill or mistery.

30

The main secret of design, as practised in the late Romanesque and early Gothic periods, consisted in the application of a module, or standard dimension, in multiples, submultiples and combinations. The modular unit itself had to be settled in accordance with the particular standard of measurements of the place, either that of the building site or that of the master's origin. In many parts of Europe during the Dark Ages the Roman foot had remained as a standard of measurement, and according to this (0·295 metre, or about $11\frac{5}{8}$ inches) some of the most important buildings were set out. At Cluny, for instance, Professor Conant has been able to demonstrate the use of a modular unit of five Roman feet (1·475 metres or 4 feet $10\frac{1}{16}$ inches). In some cases a change of unit can be demonstrated between works of different periods in the same building: at Cluny the earlier work had used a foot of greater length (0·34 metre or $13\frac{3}{8}$ inches), while in England, certainly from the twelfth century if not earlier, the standard was the royal foot still in use, equivalent to 0·305 metre and divided into 12 inches. The French *pied du roi* was longer (0·3248 metre or about $12\frac{3}{4}$ inches of the English measure). It can easily be seen that, even starting from a single system of modular geometry, individual results would differ, and that the differences would become extremely complex once the system began to be applied according to different standards of measurement. Hence it is that the very existence of such systems has been denied.

There have been many attempts to reconstruct the systems used for laying down the plan and erecting the elevation of a great mediaeval church, and these depend for the most part upon two documentary sources of late date. One of these is the commentary upon Vitruvius by the Italian editor Cesare Cesariano (1521), in which an account is given of disputes about the design of Milan 55 Cathedral in 1386 between Italian, French and German masters, used to different systems of proportion. The two main systems were known as *ad quadratum*, based upon a square, and *ad triangulum* based on the equilateral triangle. Applied to the cross-section of a church, the system *ad triangulum* naturally resulted in a lower, more squat, proportion of height to width; it was this system which was regarded as normal by the Italian masters in the fourteenth century. The other document is far more explicit: it consists in a manuscript *Compendium of Architecture* of 1681, written by Simón García, a 15

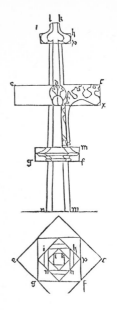

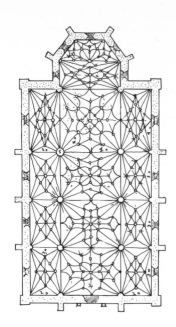

14, 15 Two late survivals of the mediaeval masonic tradition. *Left:* instructions for the design of pinnacles by Matthäus Roritzer, 1486 – elevation and plan. *Right:* a church plan designed by the Spanish architect Rodrigo Gil de Hontañón, who died in 1577, but whose drawings formed part of a treatise published in 1681

Spanish architect of Salamanca. In his own work García luckily incorporated the rules of the Gothic builders which had come down to him in an earlier manuscript compiled by Rodrigo Gil de Hontañón. Rodrigo Gil, who was already at work in 1521 and died in 1577, was the last of a notable family of Spanish architects, responsible for several of the largest cathedrals. Similar principles to those derived from the Milan discussions of 1386 and the practice of Rodrigo Gil in the sixteenth century are also found in several German treatises of the fifteenth and sixteenth, among which the best known is Matthäus Roritzer's tractate on pinnacles, published in 1486, based on the system of squares inscribed diagonally within one another.

Much nonsense has been written on the subject of mediaeval art, and several baseless ideas have gained wide currency. Among these have been the notions that all art was produced by the clergy and more especially by monks; that it was produced spontaneously by anybody, untrained but with some instinctive capacity for design and construction; and that great architecture was produced entirely without drawings. None of these views has any real foundation in fact. Though men trained as artists or as building

14

32

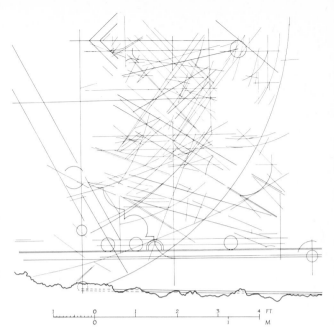

16 Part of the tracing floor above the north porch of Wells Cathedral, recorded by L. S. Colchester. The lines overlap confusingly, but the geometrical setting out of a number of architectural features can be recognized

craftsmen might, exceptionally, enter religious orders as lay brothers, or become monks, it is clear that from the eleventh century if not earlier, virtually all architecture and most sculpture was produced by laymen with a training in craftsmanship, to which literacy might be added. That, on rare occasions, there was voluntary assistance from large crowds of laymen, anxious to further some religious project, is true; but no scrap of evidence has yet been found to suggest that these 'building bees' consisted of anything more than unskilled labourers. In regard to drawings, it is quite certain that no large building, such as a cathedral, with complex interrelations between its parts, depending upon accurately shaped stones, could have been put up without at least the geometrical setting-out of its parts upon the ground. It is, in fact, very likely that the disappearance of most early constructional drawings is due to their having been traced on the ground or on a floor-slab of plaster made for the purpose. After use such drawings would be obliterated, though the plaster floors used for the purpose actually survive at Wells and York cathedrals, and an important one was in *16* use at Strasbourg until the eighteenth century.

In England, very few drawings of a technical character earlier

33

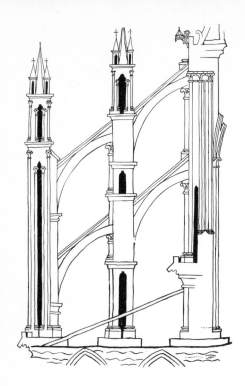

17 The most complete collection
of mediaeval drawings is the
sketch-book of Villard de
Honnecourt, a French master-
mason active between 1220 and
1235. *Left:* Villard's sketch of the
flying buttresses at Rheims

18, 19 *Right:* Villard's drawing of
one of the towers of Laon
Cathedral, with next to it a
photograph of the tower today.
'I have been to many lands', he
wrote, 'but I never saw a tower
like that of Laon.'

20–23   in date than the sixteenth century have survived, but even here there are some fragments. In France, Germany, Austria, Italy and Spain there are much larger numbers of highly finished construc-tional drawings and details, from the thirteenth, fourteenth and fifteenth centuries, many of them of outstanding excellence. The fine quality of draughtsmanship is already noteworthy in the earliest surviving scale drawings, those of the 'Rheims Palimpsest' of the middle years of the thirteenth century. These drawings, erased and cut into pieces to form pages in a book, may well have been from the hand of Master Hugh Libergiers (died 1263), architect of the church of Saint-Nicaise at Rheims, begun by him in 1229. Although none of the fragmentary drawings which survive can actually be a design for Saint-Nicaise, the style is closely similar, and there can be no doubt of the implication that small-scale drawings on parchment of the same type had been made by Libergiers in the 1220s. As we shall see, this is confirmed by the

17, 18   famous album of Villard de Honnecourt, certainly produced in the period 1220–35.

34

The finished and highly sophisticated quality of these architectural drawings produced in the first half of the thirteenth century
is not merely of importance in itself; it is also compelling evidence
that there must have been quite a long tradition of such draughtsmanship going back before the days of Honnecourt and Libergiers.
In a certain sense, namely that far earlier drawings were made, not
merely in the Near East in post-classical times, but in Ancient
Egypt, there had been a continuous tradition of such draughtsmanship for many centuries. What now concerns us is the date of
introduction of this kind of drawing into western Europe, and its
immediate source. Drawing of some kind is always essential to the
production of architecture on a large scale, but relatively simple
designs can be set out on the ground, and the details drawn out to
their full size on a table or board. The visualization of the result
depended primarily on the mental capacity of the architect, aided
by rough sketches, not even to scale, which he might trace out with
a stick on the ground. A good deal of Romanesque architecture,
though not its latest and greatest monuments, could have been

35

produced by such methods. It was the far greater degree of accuracy in foreseeing the result, brought in with the finely cut stones of the early twelfth century, that made the intermediate stage of small-scale drawings a vital necessity. In discussing the origins of Gothic we shall see that a main factor was the introduction of Euclid's *Elements of Geometry* to the West about 1120–25 by means of translation from the Arabic version by the Englishman Adelard of Bath. Again the suggestion of direct links between the Near East and north-western Europe is associated with the movements of crusaders and the supply-route to the new Frankish states in the Levant. The new technique of architectural drawing to a small scale certainly existed in the West by 1140, but there seem to be no survivals from the drawings of the first three generations concerned.

20, 21 *Left*: west front of Strasbourg Cathedral – an original drawing by Michael Parler, about 1385, and his gallery (above rose window) as built

22, 23 *Right*: a drawing for the steeple of Ulm Minster was made by Matthäus Böblinger between 1474 and 1492, but never carried out. In the nineteenth century the drawing was discovered and the church completed

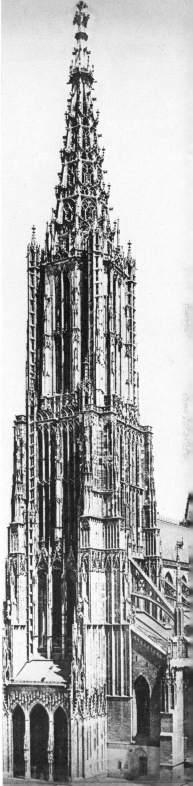

Among all the drawings of a technical character which survive, the most precious are those which form the album (so-called) of a Picard master, Villard de Honnecourt, now preserved in the Bibliothèque Nationale at Paris. Two main views have been held as to the purpose of Honnecourt's album: that it was simply the sketch-book of a mediaeval architect, filled with notes of buildings, details, and constructional devices that interested him or took his fancy; or that it was a compilation made with didactic intent for the use of a permanent building organization such as the mason's lodge of a cathedral. The modern study by Hahnloser has shown, as conclusively as is possible without direct evidence, that the latter explanation is correct. Not only are many of the drawings highly finished to a degree most unlikely in a sketch-book, but they are accompanied by lengthy written explanations. Furthermore, there are additions by later hands, at least two in addition to Honnecourt himself, and these imply continuity of use for technical purposes, rather than the mere handing down of a family possession. Again, many leaves have been cut out of the book, apparently at an early date, and this would suggest that these sections contained material regarded as valuable by some mediaeval artist who detached them to carry with him for use. That the album was in fact a sort of manuscript technical encyclopaedia of the building trades is made even more probable by the fact that many documentary references occur in mediaeval wills and other records to the existence of books of designs in the possession of master craftsmen.

The inscriptions by Honnecourt reveal still more: that he was literate and could write a very fine hand, and that he knew at least some Latin, as well as French. This is, of course, inherently likely, since mediaeval architects attached to cathedrals and the greater monasteries were in close touch with the important schools taught by the secular clergy or the monks, or by schoolmasters retained by them. Thus the building master's sons could easily obtain some book education before serving as assistants or apprentices to their fathers. That the sons of building masters were as acceptable socially as those of modern architects at the best schools is shown by the fact that among the earliest scholars of Winchester College were sons of the master mason, William Wynford, and of the master carpenter, Hugh Herland. Richard Bertie, son of the master mason of Winchester Cathedral, was admitted to Corpus Christi College,

24 The master-builder.
Peter Parler, born about
1325, took over the
building of Prague
Cathedral in 1353 and
placed his own portrait
bust in the triforium of
the choir. The Parler
family was prominent all
over central Europe.
Michael, the designer
of the Strasbourg
gallery, was Peter's
brother

Oxford, in 1534 at the age of sixteen, and after a brilliant career married the widowed Duchess of Suffolk and founded one of the greatest families in the English peerage. The educational evidence agrees with that for the relatively high social position of the mediaeval architect, who was commonly entertained at the high table of colleges and monastic houses, and ranked among the esquires of the royal household. Sometimes portraits of architects were put in places of honour in the building, as the stained-glass figures of Wynford and Herland in the chapel of Winchester College, or the bust of Peter Parler in the choir of Prague Cathedral. *24*

The architect's status

Naturally there is far more evidence concerning the architects of the later Middle Ages than for those of earlier centuries, and it might be that there had been a marked rise in status in the course of four or five centuries. What evidence there is, however, does not suggest this. Even before the Norman Conquest, the master mason Godwin Gretsyd, in charge at the building of Westminster Abbey for Edward the Confessor, was sufficiently well-to-do to be able to leave properties in Southampton to the abbey and also, along with his wife Wendelburh, to be a benefactor of Hyde Abbey at Winchester. The Norman master Robert who designed St Albans Abbey and was said to excel all the masons of his time, could give 10s. a year to the abbey funds, a sum which then (c. 1100) must have been equivalent to about £100 of the money of 1966. Later in the twelfth century Richard of Wolveston, architect to Bishop Puiset of Durham, was not only famous as a building master, but carried about in his wallet a number of painted letters of great beauty, presumably illuminated initials. This odd fact, known to us from the account of a miracle attributed to a fragment of cloth from St Cuthbert's body, placed by Master Richard along with the paintings, helps to fill out the picture of a literate and sophisticated professional man, rather than one of the rude artisans of popular imagination.

For the later Middle Ages there are detailed financial records which show what high rates of pay the greater architects could command, and the distances they were called to give advice. While it is impossible to translate mediaeval monetary values precisely into modern terms, it is not difficult to get a general idea of relative scales of pay. The masters of architectural status were paid three to four times as much as fully skilled craftsmen in their own trade. Whereas a mason or carpenter of the second half of the fourteenth century, after the Black Death, was paid wages roughly equivalent to £12 a week nowadays, a William Wynford, a Hugh Herland or a Henry Yevele would earn £3,000 a year and upwards in salary and allowances, apart from substantial profits as a contractor or maker of tombs and monuments. In the late thirteenth century Edward I's great military engineer, James of St George, was paid something like £6,000 a year, and other outstanding masters about £2,000. The French mason, Eudes de Montreuil, was getting rather more than this in the same period.

It was Eudes de Montreuil, in 1248–54, who accompanied St Louis on crusade and worked at Jaffa and in Cyprus, while in 1287 Etienne de Bonneuil went from Paris to Uppsala in northern Sweden as master mason of the cathedral, taking with him a number of assistants. All through the Middle Ages there is evidence of the employment of foreign architects and artists, and of extensive journeys undertaken, sometimes in search of materials, sometimes

40

25 Uppsala Cathedral, Sweden, built by a French architect who came from Paris in 1287

to inspect existing buildings relevant to a new design. Many consultations are on record, when architects from great distances were brought together to solve difficult technical problems. Twelve architects, some coming from distances of well over a hundred miles, assembled at Gerona in Spain to give advice in 1416 on the best design for the nave, and in central Europe the masons of the Empire were organized on a continental scale, and travelled up to 250 miles to attend periodical congresses of their craft. The rapid spread of stylistic changes is thus not difficult to explain.

Apart from the false picture of mediaeval building methods that has grown up, more general ideas of life in the period are often inadequate. This is largely due to the nineteenth-century notion of continuous progress: it is well known from many sources that European home conditions in the seventeenth and eighteenth centuries were highly insanitary, and that the roads were mostly in a deplorable condition, making travel difficult and slow; hence it was assumed that the state of affairs in the Middle Ages had been much worse. This was a fallacy, for it has been established that the greater cities of the Gothic period did much to establish paved streets, water-supply, public sanitation and municipal hygiene. Travel, on roads adequate for riding horses and mules, was not unduly difficult and was far more frequent and extensive than has been supposed. It need not be cause for amazement, then, to learn that designs for buildings were carried far and wide and across frontiers, and that even in an age without printing or any form of technical news-sheets, architects could be well informed. There were compensating factors, such as the absence of artistic copyright. The great designs for major buildings, drawn out on skins of parchment, such as can still be seen at Strasbourg and Vienna, could be and were copied, and used as the models for other works at a distance. Thus the perforated masonry spires of Burgos Cathedral in Spain, designed in 1442 by the German master Hans from Cologne (Juan de Colonia), were based upon the drawings for the western steeples of Cologne: not actually built until 1880, when the work was completed from the original designs, which had in the meantime been lost and later rediscovered.

Two social institutions in particular led to extensive travel: pilgrimage, which induced very many persons to spend long periods on journeys to Rome, to Jerusalem, to Santiago de Compostela or, to take an English example, to Canterbury; and wander-years, when a young craftsman just out of his apprenticeship would spend three years on jobs at a distance from his place of training, and often in foreign countries. Many of the names of foreign craftsmen preserved in account rolls are doubtless those of young men on their wanderings, and it must not be overlooked that even more foreigners were employed than the names would suggest, for in all countries names tended to become naturalized, as Hans von Köln in Spain became Juan de Colonia. Very frequently it is now impossible to distinguish the foreigners with any certainty.

Instead of thinking of Europe in the Gothic age as a patchwork quilt made up of the separate kingdoms and principalities, and divided by almost insurmountable barriers, we should imagine it as a relatively united and unified world in which, even in times of war, there was much travel and a general awareness of what was happening in Christendom as a whole. Nor was Christendom itself the limit of Western culture, for not only did science depend very largely upon retranslations of ancient authors made from Arabic versions, but a great deal of the mechanical invention of the period was brought from the Far East and ultimately from China. The contacts between Western Christians and Muslims, in Spain, in Sicily, and in the Levant, and the trade-route opened up across Asia by the friars and Marco Polo, were vital to the continued flow of ideas.

It can hardly be a mere coincidence that the technical revolution which ushered in the Gothic period in architecture was contemporary with the introduction to the West of Euclid's *Elements* in translation by Adelard of Bath. Adelard travelled in Spain, Italy, and through North Africa and Asia Minor, lived for a time in Sicily, and had returned to England by 1130, when he was receiving a pension from Henry I. His translations and treatises, based on the works of classical and Arabian philosophers, formed the foundation of modern science, and were soon reinforced by the productions of the school of translators of Toledo, whence versions of Aristotle made from the Arabic were issuing about 1150. Thus it is that a new art coincided with a new outlook and a phase of renewed learning. The Gothic cathedrals expressed in concrete form far more than their Carolingian or Romanesque predecessors.

43

26 *Left:* Burgos Cathedral, Spain. The Cathedral itself had been built in the thirteenth century in a predominantly French Gothic style. But the light openwork spires were added by a German architect, Hans of Cologne (Juan de Colonia) in 1442

27 The spires of Cologne (*right*) served as Hans's model, though, like Ulm, they existed then only as drawings. Until the nineteenth century Cologne Cathedral stood as a gaunt fragment; the rediscovery of the drawings in 1817 enabled it to be accurately completed

One of the profound changes which most clearly separates the quality of Gothic art from the Romanesque is an emphasis upon individuality. It is true that some degree of individual quality in design can be recognized at all periods, yet in certain cultures such as the Byzantine it was subordinated to strict adherence to rules and formulae. This implies that in the Byzantine world, as to a lesser degree in the Romanesque period in western Europe, ancient tradition was recognized as something on a higher level than what could be attained by modern man on his own. A startling reversal of outlook comes in with the Gothic style: no canonical rules bound the new art within a straitjacket, and the masters exhibited their powers of invention to the full, though borrowing ideas from one another. Instead of slowly running down, propelled by the

44

28 A selection of English masons' marks. Masons carved their mark to show responsibility for work done. There is no way of connecting them with named masons but they can prove contemporaneity of work

stored momentum of a former Golden Age, art began to be activated from within and to gather speed as it took on a form radically different from anything hitherto seen. The responsible masters, furthermore, were recognized as persons of outstanding distinction, and during the twelfth century signatures of individual artists abound. We cannot now identify the earliest generation of Gothic designers by name, but the separate styles of many men have been recognized.

The lodge and its members

Perhaps only a sculptor, but possibly also an architect, was the first great individualist in twelfth-century art, the Gislebertus who signed the tympanum of the western portal of Saint-Lazarus at Autun. Gislebert, as has been shown by Professor George Zarnecki, worked at Vézelay as well as Autun, and had probably trained on the works at Cluny; his *floruit* can be put at *c*. 1115–40, the very moment when Gothic elements (such as the sharply pointed arcades of Autun) make their first appearance in the West. Among the craftsmen who worked on the royal portal of the west front of Chartres Cathedral, in about 1145–50, was a *Rogerus artifex* who likewise signed his work, and who had very likely worked previously on Abbot Suger's church at Saint-Denis. From its opening years, the Gothic period was an age, not of anonymity, but of sharply defined and emphasized identity.

A particular sign of identity, parallel to that afforded by heraldry among the knightly class but without social significance, was the

29

46

29 'GISLEBERTUS (M?) HOC FECIT': the signature of a great mediaeval artist, at Autun; the worn letter is probably M (for *Magister*)

mason's mark. Found from remote antiquity down to modern times, the banker-marks or personal signs indicating that a particular mason cut a specific stone are of frequent occurrence in the Gothic period. Such marks are quite distinct from the position-marks, generally numerals of some kind, cut upon stones prepared at the quarry to enable them to be erected according to a diagram, course by course. The banker-mark indicates individual responsibility for work done, and is most often found where very numerous masons, strangers to one another and to the master in charge, were brought together to carry out some large operation. Some marks, and especially those of the late Romanesque and Transitional periods, were very simple, and must have been allotted again and again to gangs of men. At a given job marks of this simple kind, crosses and stars, were enough to distinguish the output of one man from that of another; but duplication of a mark must have been frequent, and have led to confusion. Later it seems that there was some degree of official control among masons, for in 1844 members of the British Archaeological Association were told by one of the elder masons at Canterbury Cathedral that his own mark had belonged to his father and grandfather before him, and that 'his grandfather had it from the lodge'. It was also stated that when a stranger joins in work with other men, one of whom has a mark similar to his, the 'foreigner' 'has to apply to his lodge for a fresh mark', but on leaving that set of workmen may resume his former sign. This evidence of traditional usage is important, and helps to explain the observed facts. In many cases it appears that marks similar but not identical (that is, 'differenced' like heraldic charges) were adopted by members of the same family or by pupils of a master. Very few marks, however, can be attached to the names of their users, and no written register of marks seems to have survived from the Middle Ages.

There is not much evidence to suggest that the masons' 'lodge' of the Middle Ages had any of the esoteric significance attached to the lodges of modern speculative Freemasonry. The lodge was a

47

workshop and shelter, and might be a permanent building in which there was a floor-slab of plaster for setting out the details of the work, as well as a drawing-office provided with trestle tables or drawing-boards of some kind. Administratively, the 'lodge' was also a courthouse and the body of men assembled in it, under the control of the master mason, maintained discipline and upheld the regulations of the masons' craft. These are known from manuscripts which have come down from the fourteenth and fifteenth centuries, setting forth a traditional history of the mason's craft as well as the series of regulations known as the Articles and Points of Masonry. It is of interest that the traditional history, containing both mythical statements as to the earliest origins of the craft in Old Testament times, and the attribution of geometry to Euclid, can be traced back, as regards some of its elements, to the first quarter of the twelfth century. This is what would be expected on the supposition that the beginning of the system of building organization was in fact the introduction of Gothic elements into western Europe.

Apart from the reference to Euclid and the equation of geometry with the mason's craft, the manuscripts state that the rise of masonry was due to 'great lords' children freely begotten' and forbid a master to take any apprentice born of bond blood. Even allowing for exaggeration, there can be no doubt that mediaeval masons enjoyed a relatively high social status, and that this tended towards the creation of an architectural profession, whose members were regarded as practising a liberal art rather than a base skill. High status was also implied by the mediaeval iconography of God *30* the Father as Creator, designing the Universe with a pair of compasses: the concept of 'the Great Architect of the Universe' goes back far beyond the modern expression of the idea.

In various forms there was highly developed organization of the mason's craft in Europe. Throughout the Empire, and indeed beyond it, there existed a widespread jurisdiction under the control of the Master of the Strasbourg Lodge, with subordinate regions directed from Berne, Cologne and Vienna, which extended its rule over the whole of Hungary as well as the Austrian duchies. There is positive evidence that congresses were held in the late fourteenth and fifteenth centuries, attended by representative masters from an area nearly five hundred miles across. In such

48

30 God the Father, the Great Architect of
the Universe, from a thirteenth-century
French Bible

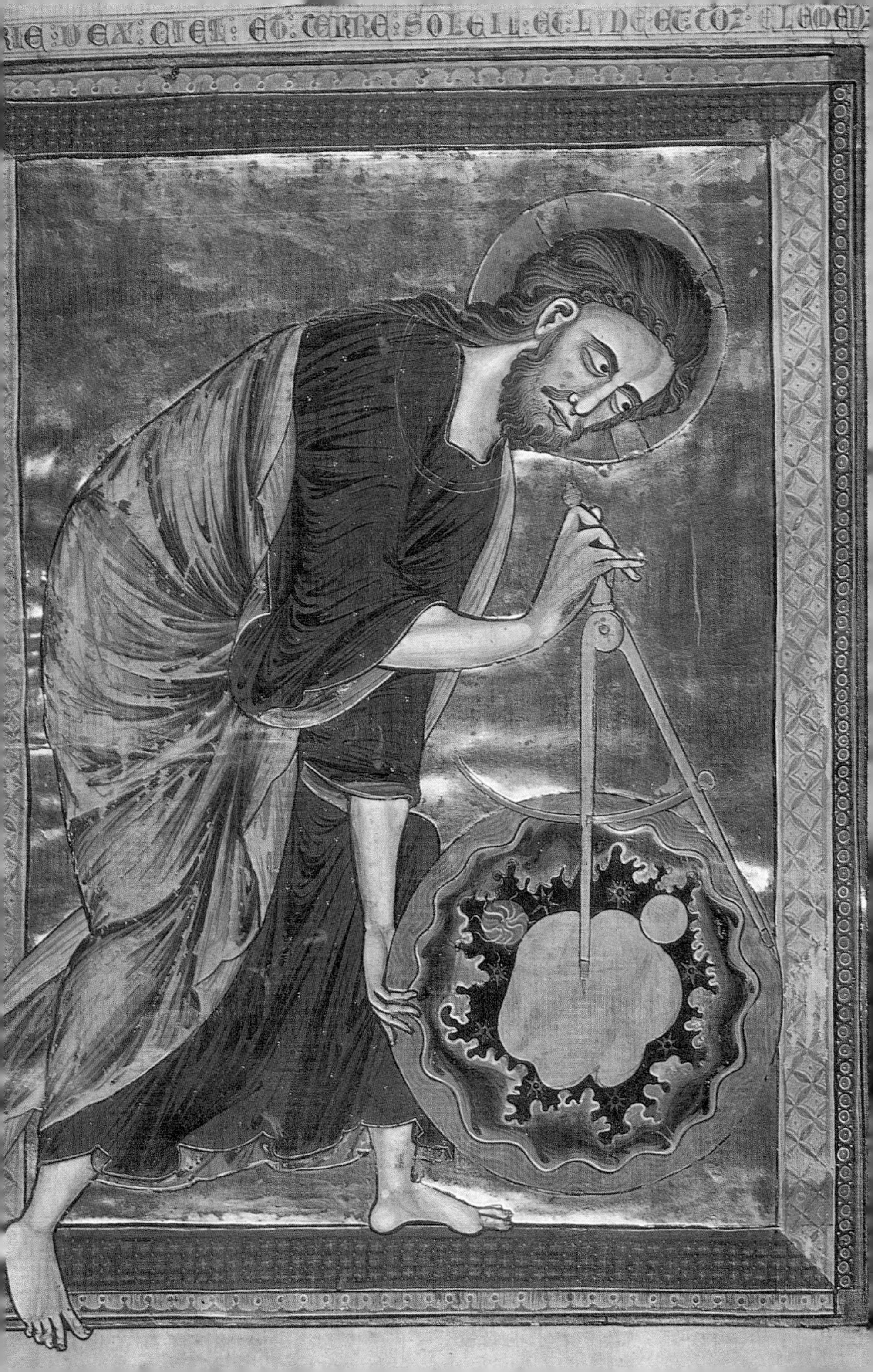
RIE : DEX : CIEL : ET : TERRE : SOLEIL : ET LVNE ET TOZ ELEMEN

circumstances new fashions in architecture were rapidly carried over wide distances, and the revolutionary art of the Parler family, for instance, spread over the whole of central Europe within a century.

In France the mastery over the masons had been the subject of a royal grant before 1268, and in England the king's master mason certainly exerted considerable influence on style, even though he had no formal control over masons throughout the country. There were local assemblies of masons of some kind, and according to the early masonic constitutions these were presided over by civic officials, the sheriffs of counties or the mayors of towns. In 1305 Walter of Hereford, one of the chief masters of Edward I, was granted the continuance of his right to hold his 'free Court' over the workmen at Caernarvon Castle, with the fines for breaches of contracts made by the subordinate craftsmen. Though the direct evidence is scanty, it is sufficient to prove that mediaeval masons did not work in any anarchistic isolation.

What is of outstanding interest is the extent of international linkage implied by the little evidence that does exist. The very long journeys undertaken by individual master masons prove that, in spite of necessarily slow communications, it was not uncommon for personal fame as an architect to cross frontiers and to reach points hundreds of miles distant. This is certain in regard to French masters in the twelfth and thirteenth centuries, and in the case of German architects of the later Middle Ages. Now in the latter instance we have just seen that this is accounted for by the known existence of a widespread organization dominated by the Master of Strasbourg. His official influence was spread by a 'network' not merely throughout the German-speaking lands of the Empire, but also in Switzerland which was no longer politically imperial, and into Hungary which had no connection with the mediaeval Empire. Looking back to the origins of this remarkable institution at Strasbourg, several more notable facts are recorded. It is stated, and there is no good reason to doubt, that in the year 1275 (i.e. at the time of the start on the west front of the cathedral) the master, Erwin 'von Steinbach', called together the most famous masters of works from Germany, from Italy and from England. This assembly is then said to have perpetuated itself by founding a lodge with autonomous jurisdiction, at once confirmed to it by the

Emperor, the Habsburg Rudolf I. The most significant statement is that the source of this permanent 'lodge' was the 'English fashion' of 'freed masonry' (i.e. masons with their own autonomous jurisdiction).

This might be regarded as a picturesque fable if it were not for the firm record of a 'free court' of masons in England already in existence before 1305, and for the more general evidence of the manuscript regulations and 'history'. It is worth noting that the date, 1275, of the imitation of English methods was just when English political influence had reached a peak on the return of Edward I from crusade. Given that adequate communications did exist, the invitation extended to English masters is intelligible. Even though such an international congress of architects may have been highly exceptional, it falls into line with the suggestion that the English masons' organization held county assemblies every year, and probably regional or provincial meetings as well, perhaps every third year.

The manuscripts which include the masonic 'history' and regulations refer to earlier books in French and Latin, from which the surviving versions were derived soon after 1350. Again the date is significant, for it was in 1350 that the language of instruction in English petty schools was changed from French to English; grammar schools, at all periods, taught mainly Latin. A coherent picture of masters from various countries, able to communicate with one another in French or in Latin, emerges. So far as England is concerned, the date of organization can be put back well before the opening of the reign of Edward I. In fact evidence of a different kind suggests that it went back very much earlier. The famous London Assizes of Building of 1189 and 1212, though in themselves municipal ordinances concerned largely with fireproof construction, imply a great deal of antecedent technical knowledge which must have been supplied by well-qualified masons. Furthermore, it is precisely the important provision that a stone party-wall sixteen feet high needs a foundation three feet wide, that is carried back further still by the 1189 Assize. This contains a historical section stating that the building of such stone walls for the most part began only after the Great Fire of London of the first year of King Stephen (1136). Once again the records go back to the epoch of the first fine ashlar masonry and of the origins of Gothic.

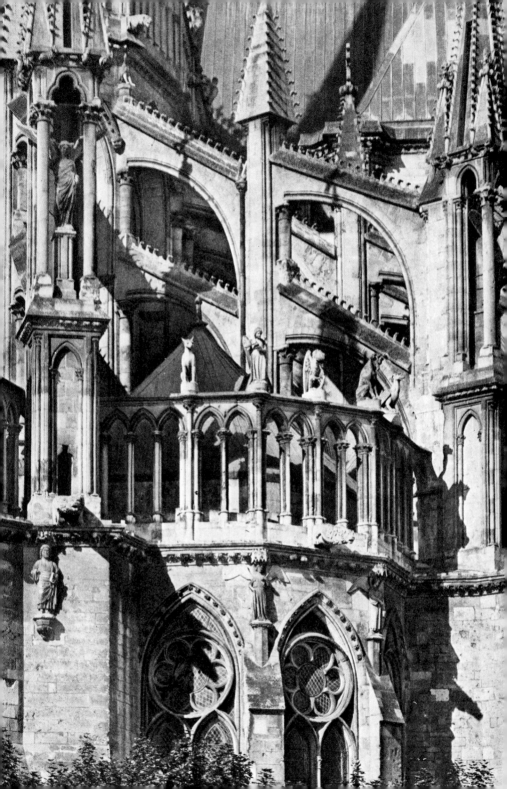

Chapter Three

The Birth of Gothic

The development of architecture through the period may be divided into three main phases. First, at the opening of the twelfth century, came the elements of Gothic style and their gradual elaboration over a period of rather more than a century. Soon after the year 1200 there was a fully co-ordinated Gothic art particularly marked by the invention of windows with bar-tracery, probably first used by Jean d'Orbais at Rheims Cathedral during the genera- *31* tion following 1211, when the east end was begun. A century of classic poise followed, in which an international architecture reached its peak and produced perfected forms of cathedral, castle and palace, enriched with painting, stained glass, patterned tiles and figure sculptures. In third place came the segregation of national styles, corresponding in some measure to political divisions. True to her insular position, England led the way in this latest Gothic epoch, followed by Germany and by the kingdoms of the Peninsula. France remained, until almost the close of the Middle Ages, conservatively attached to the earlier international aesthetic, and only slowly incorporated into its tradition the highly enriched style of late or Flamboyant Gothic which, inspired by the ogee curves adopted in England near the end of the thirteenth century, became characteristic of building in Flanders and the Low Countries and was thence carried into Spain.

The characteristics of the Gothic style in Italy differ widely from those found elsewhere. Beginning at the south, influenced as it was by Byzantine and Saracenic factors, style in Sicily was so untypical that it cannot be considered here. In southern Italy true Gothic was an alien style, a direct importation of French or Spanish forms, while in central Italy around Rome and throughout the Papal States it might be said that Gothic never existed. Only in three northern provinces, Tuscany, Lombardy and Venice, were there *55, 56, 91* genuinely Gothic styles, and their aesthetic qualities differed greatly

53

from the norm accepted elsewhere in Europe. For this reason not much of the Italian architecture of the Middle Ages belongs to the main stream of artistic development. Where Gothic in general was tall and aspiring, that of Italy was low and spacious. Profoundly permeated by the survival of Roman forms of antiquity, Italian art could never acquiesce in the extension of length or height, the sharpness, the angularity of mediaeval buildings. The dome, usually rejected elsewhere, was accepted; external colour largely took the place of the play of light and shade upon mouldings. Only in Venetian Gothic did moulding and tracery play a full and rich part.

We have seen that the first sparks of the Gothic spirit, coming from the East, reached eastern France early in the twelfth century, and that related constructional ideas had already reached England earlier still. Before 1150 architecture in a style recognizably Gothic in its elements existed at Saint-Denis, close to Paris; at Chartres Cathedral fifty miles away; and also in the Crusaders' church of the Holy Sepulchre at Jerusalem, over two thousand miles off at the far end of the Mediterranean. This architecture, consistently pointed in its arches and designed for ribbed vaults, may be contrasted with the essentially Romanesque and round-arched work hitherto current. As a complete church just beyond the point where Gothic as a style had begun, Sens Cathedral, built between 1135 and 1160, is of outstanding interest. It has further importance as the presumed place of origin of William of Sens, the French master brought to England to design the new choir of Canterbury Cathedral, begun by him in 1175–78 and continued, in more advanced style, by his assistant William the Englishman, from 1179 to 1184.

The early Gothic of the Cistercian Order, deprived by strict rule of adventitious decoration, can be seen at Pontigny (c. 1140–1210), and even better at Alcobaça in Portugal, where the great church of 1158–1223 survives entire. In Spain, too, at the Old Cathedral of Salamanca, can be seen the remarkably successful achievement of a new aesthetic within a generation or little more of the arrival of the first elements of the new style. On a magnificent scale, in France itself, is the cathedral of Laon, begun soon after the middle of the twelfth century and mostly built by 1205, though its east end was rebuilt and its towers never finished. The spreading wave of the new style reached England after the chaos of Stephen's reign

54

32 The sexpartite vault of Sens Cathedral, built between 1135 and 1160

33 The new nave of Ripon, begun about 1180, shows Gothic becoming accepted in England

had given place, in 1154, to the vigorous government of the Angevin Henry II. Within the next twenty years the elements of Gothic began to be seen in the western bays of the nave at Worcester, and in the aisleless nave of Ripon built for Archbishop Roger of York towards the end of his long episcopate (1154–81) and perhaps still later, under the mason Master Arthur, who flourished about 1190. To some degree under the influence of work done for the Cistercian Order these first attempts at insular Gothic remained transitional in character.

    Romanesque elements were first completely abandoned at Wells Cathedral, designed in or soon after 1175 and largely built by 1192. Entirely distinct from earlier work in France, and from the French style of Canterbury, the style of Wells preserves nothing of Norman solidity and massing, while exquisitely graceful carvings enrich capitals and bosses. At Wells a purely new aesthetic had made

33

34 In Spain the Gothic
tendency to replace
massiveness by strong
structural lines is first seen in
such works as the
ambulatory of Ávila
Cathedral, 1160–1200

its appearance and scored its great triumph, before spreading
through western England and South Wales, and across to the zone
of English occupation in Ireland, where Dublin had been taken in
1170. At Lincoln Cathedral also, where the choir and transepts
were built in 1192–1200, there was a great advance beyond the
Canterbury stage of work, and individual idiosyncrasies can be
seen in the wall arcading and the strange ribbed vaults.

England, for the thirty-five years of Henry II's reign the centre
of the strongest political organism of the West, had begun to
achieve that mercantile hegemony of the western seas which she
was to maintain for more than seven centuries. In research too
England was entering upon a new era of primacy. In France itself
the highest level of contemporary scholarship and culture was
attained by John of Salisbury (c. 1115–80), an Englishman of Saxon
descent (as Adelard of Bath had been), who became Bishop of
Chartres. The life of such churchmen-courtiers was spent largely
in travel and in the greater palaces of the kings and princes of their
time. Among such palaces Westminster is the chief survivor, in
96, 97 respect of its great hall, and England can show too the notable keeps

built for Henry II at Newcastle upon Tyne (1171–77) and Dover (1180–91), by the engineer Maurice. Still greater was the castle built for Richard Cœur-de-Lion at Château-Gaillard in Normandy in 1197–98.

It was not only in England that the new tendency to eliminate Romanesque solidity and to reduce supports to slender dimensions took root. This modern trend is well seen in the ambulatory of Ávila Cathedral in Spain, built between 1160 and 1200. On the other hand, some greater churches retained the Transitional style, harking back to Romanesque models which seem to peep through a Gothic veneer, and such a church, noble but conservative, is the old cathedral of Lérida in Catalonia, not built until 1203–78. A conservative adherence to much of the older style remained characteristic in France, where some degree of subservience to the Roman orders of architecture can long be noted, even in the new Chartres Cathedral begun after 1194. Still weighty and classical, Notre-Dame in Paris, begun in 1163, and the rebuilt Chartres lead on towards the more purely Gothic but still conservative Rheims (1211–90) and Amiens (1220–88). In the meantime a far more original solution of the problem of cathedral design had emerged at Bourges, begun in c. 1192. The architect of Bourges, while adhering to the essential plan of Sens and Paris, broke away from traditional treatment for the first time in France, and flung upwards immensely tall pillars surrounded by slender shafts. Though this has the effect of reducing the triforium storey to somewhat crushed proportions, the effect of soaring height appearing actually to be forcing itself towards heaven had been achieved. Of all the great cathedrals of the earliest true Gothic, Bourges is both the most original and the most successful in its internal effect. It was complete in essentials by 1225, and was followed by two others which had learned its lesson: Le Mans, built in 1217–54, and Coutances in Normandy, built in the generation from about 1220 to 1250. Coutances, a cathedral strangely neglected by the historians of art, is probably the purest example of the early maturity of Gothic style, and has for its central lantern the noblest tower ever built. The massing and external composition of Coutances are superb, and it shares with the unfinished Le Mans the distinction in its own period, of having been manifestly designed for architectonic effect, without as well as within.

34

37, 38

35, 36

39, 40, 126

41, 42

43

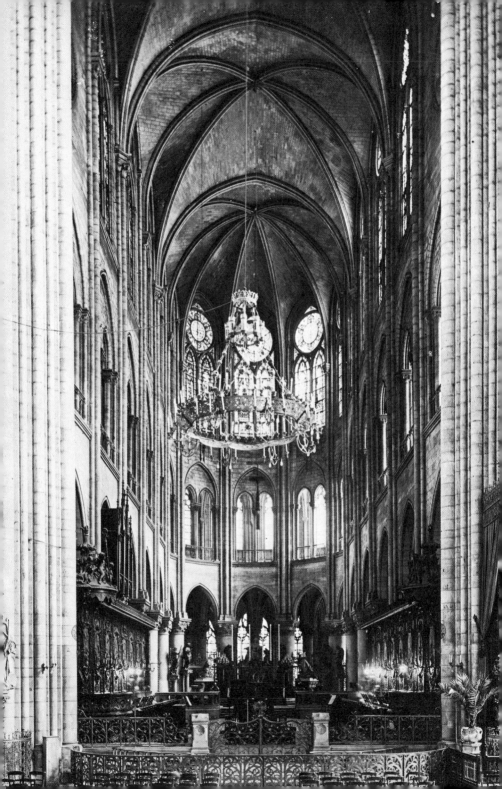

35–38 THE EVOLUTION
OF FRENCH GOTHIC
Left: Notre-Dame,
Paris, late twelfth
century. Early Gothic
elements still remain –
the round piers of the
arcade and the
sexpartite vault.
Right: by the mid-
thirteenth century, at
Amiens, a form had
been reached which
was to remain
definitive for the next
200 years –
quadripartite vault
carried on shafts
continuing to the
ground, and supported
on the exterior by a
network of flying
buttresses. The two
west fronts are shown
below. Paris retains a
static squareness,
Amiens expresses an
exultant upward
movement

39, 40 Bourges Cathedral, the west front and interior of the choir.
Bourges is so high that the aisle elevation – on the far right – has all the
elements of the main elevation of a normal cathedral

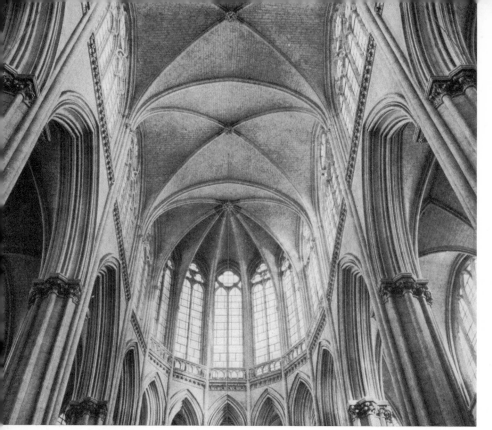

41, 42 The cathedral of Le Mans (*left*), begun in 1217, was modelled on Bourges, with tall piers, double aisles, and (*above*) quadripartite vaults

43 *Right:* Coutances, built within a single generation (1220–50) and uniquely consistent in style. This view from the east shows the elaborate exterior support for the choir vault

French designs of the earlier thirteenth century include the cathedral of Meaux and that of Troyes, begun in 1208; further to the east lay Metz, where the nave of the cathedral was started in 1239–60 though not completed until 1348. The ambitious choir of Beauvais, probably designed by Eudes de Montreuil, the master who accompanied St Louis on crusade, was put up in 1247–72, but the vaults, the highest ever built (158 feet), collapsed in 1284 and restoration lasted another forty years, under a new master, Guillaume de Roy. The fall of Beauvais must have been a landmark in the progress of mediaeval masoncraft, empiric as it was: so notable

44
45

44, 45 Two French designs of the mid-thirteenth century – Metz (*left*), begun in 1239, and Beauvais, the highest ever built, begun in 1247

46 Cologne, begun in 1248 but not completed until the nineteenth
century, carries the ideals of the French Gothic to their logical climax

a failure must have served as a valuable though costly lesson. The general design of Beauvais was echoed at Cologne, where the first stone was laid in 1248, only one year later. At Cologne the vaults rise to 150 feet, and the whole project was eventually completed, though late in the nineteenth century. It is at Cologne that we see best the intentions of the architecture of St Louis and his age.

The first Gothic cathedrals had accepted the general character of Romanesque internal design: the division into three heights, of arcade, triforium and clerestory. Characteristic of the thirteenth century was the attempt to reorganize this pattern to produce greater unity of effect. One early way of trying to achieve unity was to include the triforium in a tall arcade, as was done in the nave of St Frideswide's, Oxford, between 1158 and 1180. A similar design is found at Glastonbury Abbey, but its awkwardness must have been apparent, and future efforts were directed towards the incorporation of the triforium in the clerestory, and the linking of the horizontal stages by continuous vertical members. Both in France and England this search for unity was proceeding in the late twelfth and early thirteenth centuries.

The first traces of this search for unity in bay design are seen in a church still largely Romanesque in character: the new choir of Saint-Rémi at Rheims, built in the 1170s, with low arcades, a tall tribune, and a stunted triforium incorporated into the clerestory. No such four-storey work occurs in England, but within a few years the nave of St David's Cathedral in Wales similarly incorporated a triforium of small arches within a round-arched clerestory. The style of the Gothic features at St David's is clearly derived from Wells, not from France, and it was masons from Wells or the Bristol area who must have designed Christ Church Cathedral in Dublin. There, in the nave begun about 1213, was a fully Gothic design in which a triforium and a clerestory of adequate heights were integrated and given their full proportional value in the bay. The same scheme appeared in England at Llanthony Priory soon afterwards and at Pershore Abbey choir between 1223 and 1239; then at Southwell Minster in the period 1234–50. It is noteworthy that the strictly Gothic development of this unifying factor in design took place entirely within the West of England school, the least subject to direct influence from France and in fact showing virtually no details of French style.

66

47–49 The integration of bay
design by absorption of the
triforium
Below: Pershore Abbey, 1223–39
Right: Llanthony Priory, 1180–
c. 1210
Below right: Southwell Minster,
1234–50

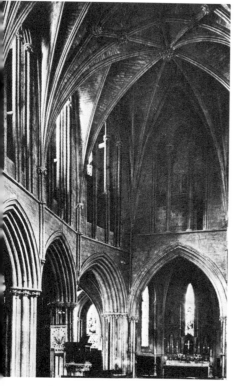

50, 51 English Gothic of the
mid-thirteenth century
stressed the clear division of
members such as shafts and
ribs, emphasizing their linear
qualities by black Purbeck
marble. Salisbury (*right*)
begun in 1220, is almost
without ornament.
Lincoln's Angel Choir (*left*),
1256–80, is enriched with
sculpture and window
tracery

In France itself, however, parallel development was taking place
under the great king's mason Pierre de Montreuil, possibly the
father of the Eudes de Montreuil already mentioned. In the rebuilding of Saint-Denis from 1231, clerestory and triforium were
linked by vertical shafting and tall shafts detached from the wall
were used by Pierre de Montreuil in such a way as to give an illusion
of movement. This idea was exploited on the south-west tower of
Coutances Cathedral, and later became the keynote of the extra-
ordinary front at Strasbourg. Such exploitation of vertical members
was one of the main features of mature Gothic, and was to lead in
England to the invention of what is known as the Perpendicular
style, the most individual and recognizable of all the national styles
of late Gothic.

68

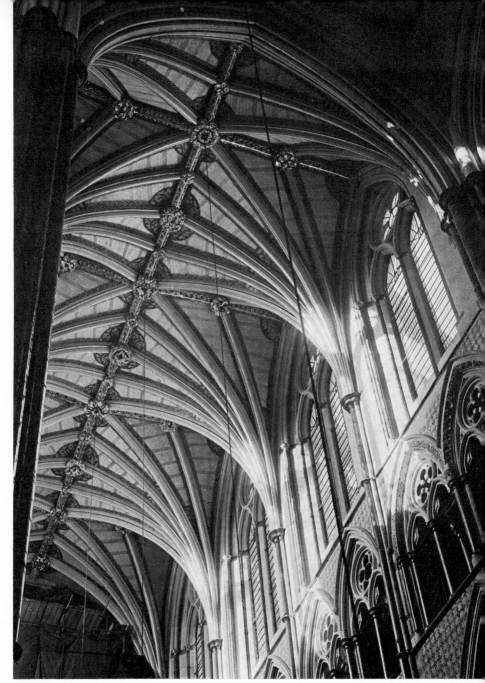

52 Westminster Abbey, begun in 1245, is strongly influenced by French
examples, but incorporates many English features, such as the ridge-rib

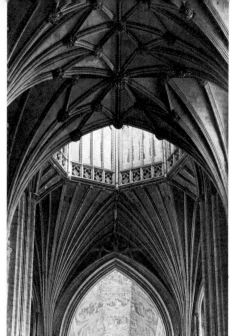

53, 54 The development of English vaulting – Lincoln nave (*left*), of about 1235, employs tiercerons; Ely choir, a hundred years later, forms a net of tiercerons and liernes

The 'classic' century

Before the coming of Perpendicular in England and of *Sondergotik*, its German derivative, another century was to elapse. It was in this hundred years, from the first third of the thirteenth century onwards, that the great culmination of the 'classical' Gothic style took place. In England, where the true Gothic had been ushered in at Wells, slender verticality reached a peak in the lady chapel of Salisbury Cathedral (1220–25). The rest of the cathedral followed without a break and was completed, except for the central tower and spire, by 1266. The nave of Lincoln Cathedral, where patterned vaulting of a perfected type appears for the first time, was built between 1220 and 1237, and its design was almost immediately adopted in the new presbytery at Ely, built between 1234 and 1250. A later phase of thirteenth-century English style, influenced to some extent by French models, begins with King Henry III's rebuilding of Westminster Abbey from 1245, and appears at Lincoln in the noble Angel Choir of 1256–80.

51

53

52
50

Developments on the Continent included the building of Siena 56
Cathedral in Italy, in the half-century after 1226, and the start of
work, in 1227, of the Metropolitan cathedral of Spain at Toledo. 129
Though inspired by French models and perhaps laid out by a French
master, the Martin mentioned by several documents, Toledo
Cathedral initiated a Spanish type of greater church. Far less high

55, 56 Italian Gothic is a separate story from that of the north: Milan
(*left*), begun in 1387, and (*below*) the west front of Siena Cathedral,
designed by Giovanni Pisano about 1284

than the French models, it shows the Peninsular tendency to spread in area and to proliferate in side chapels. On the other hand, León Cathedral is almost wholly French in character and was largely built between 1255 and 1277, when the master Enrique de Burgos died. He may well have come from France before 1235, when he had taken up the work of Burgos Cathedral, already begun in 1221.

57 Both at Burgos and at León, Enrique (Henri?) was succeeded by a Spanish master, Juan Pérez. As with the English Henry of Reyns (Rheims?), who worked for Henry III from 1243 at Windsor, Westminster and York, we have here an instance of the architect-mason who had control over jobs in widely separated places. Such men were a commonplace by the 1260s, when the Dominican friar Nicholas de Biard preached a sermon now famous in the annals of art history. Bishops, said de Biard, were like those master masons who, wearing gloves and holding a measuring-rod, say to others: 'Cut it for me this way', doing no labour yet getting higher pay. In another discourse he challenged those prelates who worked by word alone, like the chief masters then usual at great buildings, who ordain by word, rarely or never set their hands to the work, and are paid more than anyone else.

By this time we know the names of a large proportion of the great architects responsible for the outstanding churches, castles and royal palaces of Europe. Salisbury was begun by Nicholas of Ely; the nave of Wells completed by Adam Lock (who died in

59
60 1229) and its glorious west front carried out by Thomas Norreys and the sculptor Simon; at Durham the eastern Chapel of Nine Altars was built by Richard Farnham from 1242; Master Sampson was engaged at Ely between 1240 and 1274; the architect of Lichfield was one Thomas at the time the transepts were built and the chapter-house designed, in 1220–50; at Lincoln and at Worcester the works were controlled by the great master Alexander, who succeeded at Lincoln to one Michael, and was in his turn replaced

50 by Simon of Thirsk, who built the Angel Choir. At Cologne the original architect of 1248, a man obviously very well informed as to French work at Amiens and Beauvais, was Master Gerhard. His contemporary in France, Jean des Champs, trained on the building of the Sainte-Chapelle at Paris, went south to start a new cathedral at Clermont-Ferrand in 1262, and thus opened a fresh chapter in the history of French Gothic style.

74

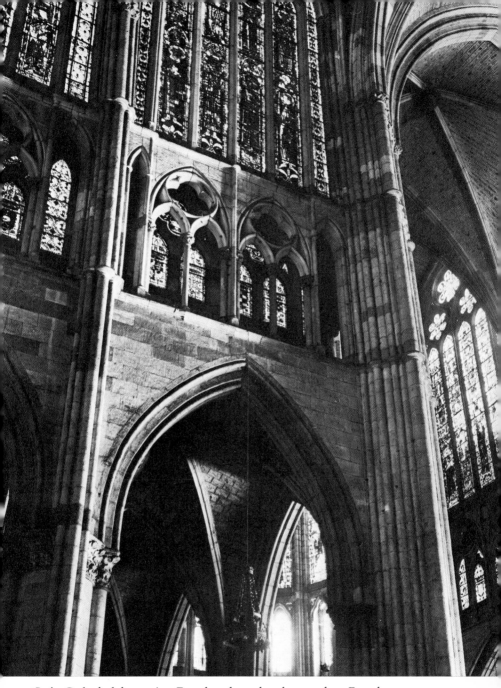

57 León Cathedral, begun in a French style, and perhaps under a French master in 1255, was continued by the Spaniard Juan Pérez

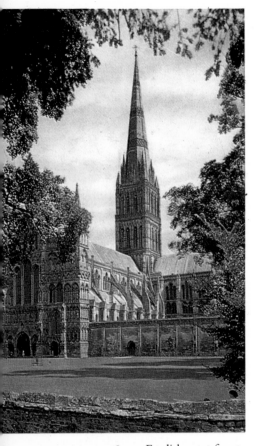

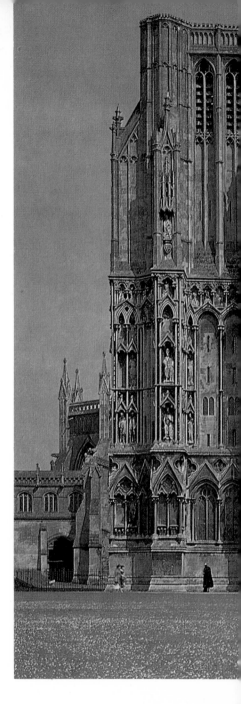

58, 59 English west fronts. Both Salisbury (*above*) and Wells (*right*) use the west front as a screen for the display of sculpture. Wells is unique in preserving nearly all its original figures

60 The Chapel of
the Nine Altars,
Durham, was begun
in 1242 in order to
provide more space
for altars at the east
end of the cathedral.
The architect's name
is known: Richard
Farnham

61 *Right:* chief
architectural sites of
the thirteenth
century

In the south of France the character of the greater churches had
hitherto differed greatly from the northern style of Normandy,
Paris and Champagne. Wide churches of a single span, or of hall
type, with aisles of equal height, and sometimes buttressed by
ranges of side chapels, were normal in the whole of the southern
regions bordering on the Mediterranean and in the centre of the
country. Starting with Clermont-Ferrand and pushing on to
Limoges (begun in 1273), to Narbonne and the choir of Toulouse,   62
both started in 1272, and to Rodez, whose cathedral was begun five
years later, Jean des Champs carried the new wave of design to the
limits of the country. Meanwhile, in the North, still further advances in style were being made in the transepts of Amiens (*c.* 1270–
88) and the splendid west front of Rheims, built by Bernard de   63

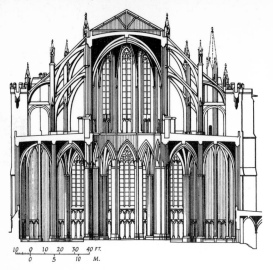

62 The choir of Narbonne Cathedral (*left*) shows the Île-de-France style being carried to the south-west of France during the late thirteenth century

63 Detail of the west front of Rheims, designed by Bernard de Soissons and built between *c.* 1255 and 1290

Soissons between about 1255 and 1290. In what was then western Germany, the designs for Strasbourg were being made, and its west front begun in 1276. Though greatly influenced by French precedents, all the Strasbourg masters were Germans: Rudolf the elder, who was building the south transept in the 1230s and the nave between 1250 and his death in 1276; Erwin von Steinbach, who built the front to the top of the great rose window in 1276–1318; and his sons and nephews who completed the towers by 1365. The northern steeple, added later in the period of *Sondergotik*, was likewise carried out by Germans, Ulrich von Ensingen who built the octagon (1399–1419) and Johann Hültz, who finished the spire in 1439.

Diverging styles

By the last decade of the thirteenth century a great turning-point had been reached. Gothic style had until that time been entirely dominated by the inventions of masters who either worked in France or had their origins there. To this there is a partial exception in the early Gothic of the English West Country school, sharply independent of the French introductions at Canterbury, Chichester or Lincoln. It must be remembered, too, that there were two utterly different ruling styles within France itself: that of the north, too commonly regarded as the only 'Gothic', and the very different and more spacious style of the South and West, with related works in Italy, in eastern Spain and, occasionally, in England, as at the Temple Church choir in London finished in 1239. French masters travelled

80

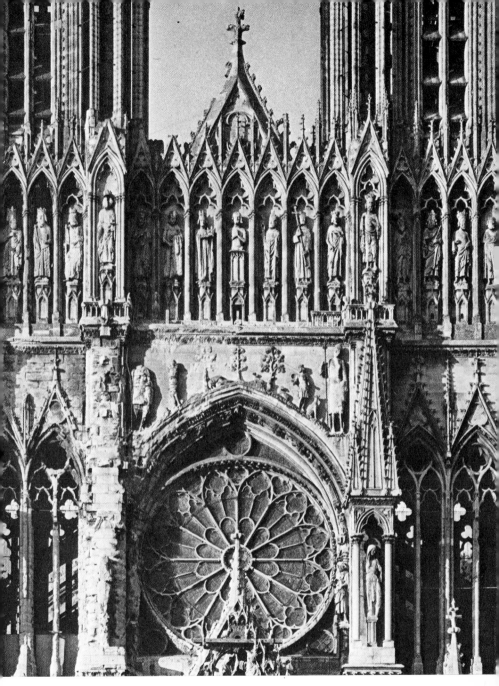

to England and across Europe; to northern Scandinavia and to southern Italy; to Spain in the west and to Cyprus and Palestine in the east. Villard de Honnecourt's known journeys took him from Saint-Quentin in Picardy to Laon and Rheims, to Lausanne in Switzerland and across Austria to Hungary and back.

England, which in Norman times had excelled France itself in the number and scale of its churches and castles, built for the energetic dynasty of the Conqueror, had descended into political anarchy by the time that early Gothic was making its appearance. It was the renewed domination of the West by Edward I (1272–1307) that saw England once more able to forge ahead and to take the lead, this time decisively, not only for herself but in respect of the course to be taken by architecture over most of Europe for the next two hundred years. As at the opening of the Romanesque and Gothic periods, a new age of development began with the arrival of fresh ideas brought from the East. During the thirteenth century the appalling menace of the Mongol hordes had swept westward and then receded, to be replaced by at first uneasy and then relieved relations between the West and the immense and peaceful dominions of the Great Khan. Once more the products of Oriental invention were brought to Europe by merchants and returning travellers. The Mongols, broad-minded pagans, were seen as a field of missionary activity and as allies against the Muslims.

The western dominions of the Mongols, centred in Persia, were ruled by a viceroy called the *ilkhan*, and Arghun, *ilkhan* from 1284 until 1291, cultivated relations with the Christian states and sent embassies to the West, including one which reached London in 1289. Edward I sent a return mission to Persia under Sir Geoffrey Langley, who had been on crusade with him in 1270–74, and this mission went by way of Constantinople and Trebizond to Tabriz in 1292, returning in the following year. In that same year, 1293, Christian missionaries from Italy reached China, and in 1295 Marco Polo with his father and uncle returned safely to Venice from Peking. That such contacts with the East actually affected Western buildings is shown by the instance of the great hall of the Palazzo della Ragione at Padua, designed by Frate Giovanni, an Austin friar, in 1306. He had travelled widely in Europe and Asia and 'brought back plans and drawings of all the buildings he had seen'. Among his drawings was one of the roof of 'a great palace in India beyond the sea', which Brother Giovanni used as his model in designing the enormous timber roof at Padua, which covers an area of 240 by 84 feet.

The embassy of Sir Geoffrey de Langley included a certain *Robertus sculptor*, who may well have been another artist equipped with a sketch-book. Certain it is that during the last years of the thirteenth century new motives in pattern appear in England, and closely resemble Persian diaperwork. The ogee arch, formed of S-curves, was also exploited in England before 1300, and was probably used still earlier in Venice. That a form so characteristic of later Gothic should be found in western Europe at first precisely in Venice and in England strongly supports the derivation of the motive from those Oriental contacts which were common to both mercantile societies. The unusual north doorway of the porch of St Mary Redcliffe at Bristol, paralleled in the West only by the *64, 65* related polygonal openings in Bristol Cathedral and at Berkeley Castle, and dating from not later than the first quarter of the fourteenth century, is the most notable instance in the whole of western Europe of the impact of Oriental ideas before the arrival of the Portuguese Manueline style (1495–1521) incorporating motives *66, 109* from the Indies. At Bristol the Redcliffe porch is itself a hexagon in plan, echoing the dominant polygon found in the new style of diapered pattern, and also the plan of the Eleanor Cross at Waltham, built in 1291–94.

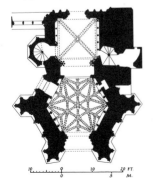

64, 65 The north porch of St Mary Redcliffe, Bristol, is unusual in its hexagonal plan and in the strange profile of the doorway, suggesting Eastern contacts

66–68 VARIETIES OF TRACERY

Left: the cloister of Batalha, Portugal, 1500, represents the end of the Gothic tradition, mingling with exotic influences from abroad.

Right: rose window in the south transept front of Amiens, climax of the French *flamboyant* style

Right: the 'Bishop's Eye' at Lincoln, *c.* 1330 – English Decorated at its most inventive

    The possibilities of the ogee curve in unifying the dissociated circles of geometrical tracery patterns were soon realized, and a

67   widespread use of 'reticulated' tracery in windows and as decoration was the result. This style had a vogue of some fifty years in England before it was driven out by the advance of the Perpendicular style, but it was taken up on the Continent and, in France and Flanders, was still further developed into the twisted and

68   writhing shapes described as *flamboyant*. To this extent the later course of the Gothic style in Europe, even in France itself, was determined by events in England. In England, however, a change of a profoundly different kind was shortly to take place, the invention of the Perpendicular style. This, though like all other styles based upon and influenced by its forerunners, must be regarded as a specifically new creation, produced about 1330 by William Ramsey, a master mason from a Norwich family who was in time to be the king's chief mason south of Trent, from 1336 until he died in London during the Black Death of 1349.

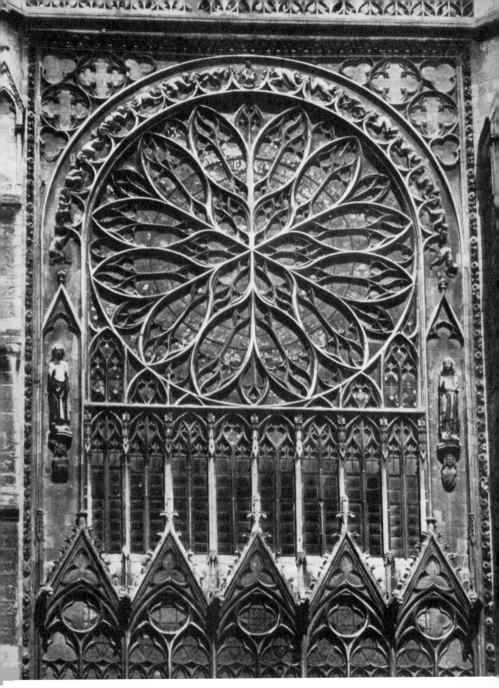

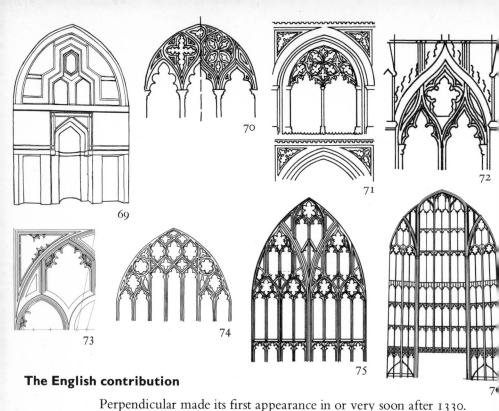

69

70

71

72

73

74

75

7

The English contribution

Perpendicular made its first appearance in or very soon after 1330.
The simplicity and even starkness of the new style, its rigid verticals
and horizontals, have often been attributed to poverty and lack of
skill subsequent to the Black Death of 1348–49, when so many of
the older generation of artists died. It is now quite certain that no
such causal connection could have existed, for the essential features
of the new style were in being quite fifteen years before the pesti-
lence. The earliest signs of Perpendicular motives are related to
reticulated pattern, which comes to be laterally compressed so that
each reticulation tends to develop, instead of continuous curves,
straight vertical sides. This process in design is seen first in works
with which William Ramsey was associated, the south cloister of
70, 77 Norwich Cathedral designed about 1324, and the new cloister and
chapter-house for St Paul's Cathedral in London begun by him in
75 1332. On a grand scale the motive appears in the south window of
the transept of Gloucester Cathedral. The transept, built in *c.* 1331–
36, had not otherwise employed this specific motive, which seems
to be a stylistic afterthought, to be dated not earlier than *c.* 1335.

86

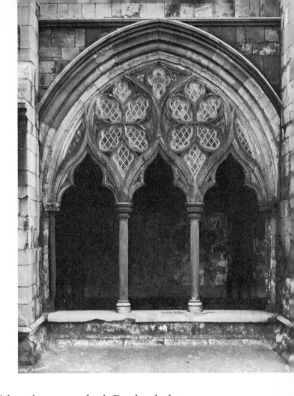

69–77 STAGES IN THE
EVOLUTION OF
PERPENDICULAR.
Islamic buildings of the
thirteenth century, such as
the tomb of Mustafa
Pasha in Cairo (69), had
reduced tracery to straight
hexagons, and English
architects probably knew
this. The south cloister of
Norwich (70 and photo
right) and Ely choir (71)
date from the 1320s; Ely
Lady Chapel (72), the
cloister of Old St Paul's
(73), Wells east window
(74) and Gloucester south
transept (75) from the
1330s. By the time of
Gloucester east window
(76) *c.* 1351 the evolution
is complete

Whence, at this time, could ideas have reached England that
would so far tend away from the main line of Gothic progress?
Again, it seems likely that the inspiration came from the East. Something very closely akin to the earliest 'squeezed hexagons' of Perpendicular tracery is found in Muslim buildings in Egypt dating from
the early thirteenth to the early fourteenth century. Associated with
other features of Perpendicular character, such as vertical members
running up to cut the curve of an arch, these forms are found in
Cairo in the Mausoleum of Mustafa Pasha (1269–73). That pilgrims,   *69*
including artists, were visiting Egypt within the relevant period is
shown by the itinerary of Simon Simeon and Hugh the Illuminator,
Franciscans from Ireland who went to the Holy Land in 1323. It is
not without interest that the unique manuscript of this narrative
first belonged to Simon Bozoun, Prior of Norwich in 1344–52, and
though such a travel-book could not itself have influenced the
course of art, it may be significant that documents of this kind were
collected at major cathedral monasteries like Norwich.

The English Perpendicular style was never adopted outside its

87

own country, apart from a few buildings designed by English architects in Scotland, Ireland and Calais. Two slightly earlier developments were, however, exported. One of these was the 'babewyne' or grotesque animal carved or painted, apparently an English speciality of the first generation of the fourteenth century. Where such grotesques are found abroad, they seem usually to be the work of travelling English artists, as in the case of Santes Creus in Catalonia, where the remarkable series of carvings in the cloister was made in 1332–51 by an English mason called 'Reinard Fonoll'

78–80

(Reginald Fenell?). Fonoll's works in Spain are completely English in style and fully confirm the statement in the records that he was from England; what is more, he arrived in Spain about 1321, and immediately practised in a style that would have been up to date at home. It is astonishing to find similar babewyneries engraved in metal at Mosul in Iraq by 1333, the date of the 'April bowl' preserved at Konya, a gift to the mother-house of the Whirling Dervishes. Possibly another English artist, captured when on pilgrimage, executed the work while a prisoner of war.

78–80 The cloister of Santes Creus (1332–51), in Catalonia, contains grotesque carvings, or 'babewynes', by an English sculptor called 'Reinard Fonoll'. A detail (*above*) shows the Lazy Mason, with maul and chisel, about to be tossed by a bull. *Below:* curvilinear tracery in the cloister. *Left:* view of the church and cloister

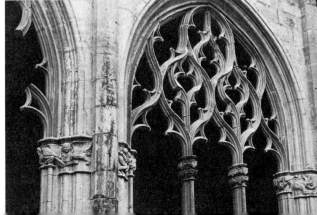

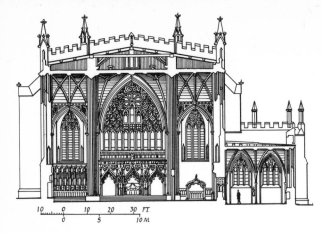

81–83 Bristol Cathedral (*left*) is one of the few English examples of a hall church, the thrust from the nave vault being carried across the aisles by ingenious masonry bridges (*right*). This type of conceit clearly pleased the Bristol master – in the vestibule to the Berkeley Chapel (*far right*) he made a vault of ribs only

A more important part was played by English inventions in vaulting. The original ribbed vault, characteristic of the first Gothic buildings, had consisted of a single pair of diagonal ribs, crossing each other at the centre of the bay. In France this form of vault was retained until near the close of the Middle Ages, though alongside other forms, some of which had a regional derivation outside the area of the main stream of Gothic style. Thus the domical vaults of western France, originating in the Angevin dominions, differed not only in their centre rising high above the lateral and transverse arches limiting the bay, but in having intermediate ribs. These additional ribs ran along the vault and across it at right angles, making angles of 45° on plan with the main diagonal ribs and thus splitting up the vault surface into eight sectors. Further subsidiary ribs were added later, by the opening of the thirteenth century.

It seems certain that English architects, aesthetically attracted by the patterns formed by such a multiplicity of ribs, deliberately adopted them for the sake of pattern. At Lincoln by the end of the twelfth century the choir vault had a longitudinal rib along the ridge, and this feature was adopted at Worcester by 1224 and was thereafter a mark of English influence. Additional (tierceron) ribs

53 begin with the Lincoln nave-vault designed about 1225–30 and soon afterwards appeared in the south transept at Lichfield and the

54 presbytery of Ely. Already English enrichment of vault surfaces had gone far beyond what was customary abroad, but early in the fourteenth century it underwent a further development. Vaults deliberately designed to form patterns were being produced before 1320.

90

The patterns can be classified under two main headings: the star-vault, in which additional short ribs were introduced between the main ribs to produce star shapes; and the net-vault, in which the ribs of the vault itself were interrupted so as to form lozenges and triangles, often breaking the continuity of the ridge-ribs and transverse ribs. The earliest star-vault known seems to be that in the crypt of St Stephen's Chapel in Westminster Palace, built about 1320, while net-vaults were used in the extraordinary hall choir of Bristol, begun about 1311. Later in the fourteenth century came the *81, 82* exclusively English fan-vault perhaps first in the chapter-house at Hereford, now ruined, and then in the cloisters of Gloucester, about *84* 1370.

A fourth English peculiarity in vaulting was the skeleton-vault, in which the vault itself with its attached ribs was supported upon a separate series of detached ribs comparable to the frame of an umbrella. First found on a very small scale in the miniature Easter Sepulchre in Lincoln Cathedral, built about 1300, such flying-ribs appear only a few years later in the vestibule to the Berkeley Chapel *83* at Bristol, and on a large scale in the choir-vault of St Mary's, Warwick, dateable to 1381–91. Both the net-vault and the skeleton-vault were copied by German masters of the fourteenth century, and became integral parts of the new style of continental practice carried across central Europe by the architects of the Parler dynasty. The masterwork of this school was to have been the cathedral of Prague in Bohemia, begun in French style by Mathieu d'Arras in *85, 86* 1344–52, and then continued under Peter Parler. The great south *24* front of 1396–1420 contains a porch with skeleton-ribs and the

91

84 The fourteenth century in England: Gloucester cloisters contain the
earliest example of an English speciality, the fan-vault

85, 86 The fourteenth century in Bohemia: Prague Cathedral, by Peter Parler, with glazed triforium and diagonal tabernacles where the windows meet the vaulting shafts

details in many respects indicate their derivation from English practice.

Profound and puzzling questions are raised by the ultimately English origin of both the Franco-Flemish Flamboyant and the Germanic *Sondergotik*. The facts are not now in doubt: in spite of strong and even chauvinistic resistance to the evidence, the chronological priority of the English models is certain, and many of the required links, political and social as well as artistic, have been demonstrated. Within the same half-century English architects or their designs were taking abroad not merely ideas but details that had been formulated in the generation of about 1290–1320. These elements of design went to Spain, to the region of the greater

93

Netherlands (whence later they passed to France), and to the whole of the vast area of Imperial masoncraft linked to Strasbourg. Their later development owed little or nothing to English influence, and there is little indication of any continuing pressure or follow-up of the initial impetus. This would in any case be unlikely, for at the very moment that the English export of its Curvilinear style was at a peak (*c.* 1330), England herself changed course and developed a determinedly isolationist style, the Perpendicular. This, as we have seen, always remained exclusively an insular phenomenon.

It seems probable that the explanation for the dominance of English architectural ideas must be sought primarily in the field of international power-politics. The phenomenon of this particular export of ideas should not be divorced from other instances of the same sort. The obvious parallel is to the earlier acceptance, by all western Europe except Italy, of stylistic domination from northern France. At all crucial times the periods of maximum architectural influence corresponded with the reigns of French kings who were successful in their political aims: of ruling the whole of geographical France, and of playing the leading part in the mediaeval concert of Europe. Contrariwise, when the King of France did not represent the dominant body of power, the vacuum was commonly filled by the King of England, with cultural and artistic as well as directly political results. The importance at the end of the eleventh century of Norman architecture stems from the victory at Hastings and from the triumphant modernization of government implicit in the Oath at Salisbury to William the Conqueror and the compilation of Domesday Book. No other monarch of the time was able to put a bridle upon feudalism; no other country compiled such a tax-collector's manual.

English influence, or rather the influence of the Court of England, was radiant under the first three Norman kings; suffered eclipse in the mismanagement of Stephen. The development of the first pure Gothic in England corresponded to the increasing fame of Henry II, just as John's loss of Normandy and western empire in 1204 led to two generations of subservience of English art to the impulses received from Parisian France. The prowess of Edward I as a crusader and his reputation as a just lawgiver were reflected in a readiness to accept English culture and art, and the tendency was reinforced by Edward's diplomatic contacts with Persia and other lands of the East. His marriage to Eleanor of Castile instituted a long period of close ties between England and the Peninsula, from which came other contacts with the Islamic world, more obviously commemorated in English folklore by the Morris (Morisco) dance than by Hispanic architectural detail. In the end the coming of Catherine of Aragon was to signal the adoption into Tudor architecture of the star-polygon plan seen at Windsor in Henry VII's Tower, in the windows of Henry VII's Chapel, and the turrets of Wolsey's great gate at Oxford, now Tom Tower.

The fact that architectural ideas and even details were carried by diplomatic missions is at first startling, but it is only a slight extension of the concept that ambassadors were bearers of splendid gifts. A foreign potentate might in some cases even ask for the services of a distinguished mason: there is reason to think that Ricardo, the architect of Las Huelgas near Burgos, went to Castile in the train of Henry II's daughter Eleanor, when she married Alfonso VIII in 1169. Robert the sculptor, as we saw, was a member of the mission of 1292 to Persia. By the sixteenth century there is a good deal of evidence that master craftsmen were employed as confidential agents, and there may have been two reasons for this. In the first place they belonged to the comparatively small category of men trained in professional standards and used to the strict practice of secrecy; secondly, the nature of their work was an excellent cover, besides giving them outstanding opportunities to appreciate the strength of fortifications and obtain other useful intelligence. Since mediaeval architects were in charge of castles and cathedrals, chapels and palaces, the harvest of information gained on a single journey might serve many purposes.

87 The fourteenth century in Germany produced the openwork spire, beginning with that of Freiburg-im-Breisgau of *c*. 1340

Chapter Four

Achievements of Gothic Maturity

During the later Middle Ages a certain few monuments of grand scale and quality dominated the scene and were widely imitated. Imitation was doubtless in part unconscious, but was largely due to a deliberate practice of copying. Patrons wished their own building to be modelled on some existing work which they could inspect, but they wished their own to go one better. This constant emulation led to continuous refinements upon a limited number of basic designs. It was during the fourteenth century that the great models were set up. For central Europe, apart from the immense influence exerted by Cologne and by Strasbourg there was a more southern centre at Freiburg-im-Breisgau, where the church steeple was built *c.* 1310–50. This fine tower formed the basis of many designs throughout southern Germany and Switzerland. The ambulatory of Freiburg (1354–60), designed by Hans Parler, the brother of Peter, was another epoch-making work in its region, and showed characteristics which were parallel to those of English Perpendicular, though without its detail. Another kind of German church, a hall comparable to the choir of Bristol Cathedral but with very tall windows (like those of the lady chapel at Lichfield) and moulded piers and arches without capitals, is the Wiesenkirche at Soest in Westphalia (1331–76), by Johann Schendeler.

In Spain the fourteenth century saw much activity, especially in the kingdom of Aragon and Catalonia. Barcelona Cathedral was begun in 1298 and the transept completed by 1317; in the next twelve years the chevet was built under the great master Jaime Fabre, who was probably responsible also for the impressive cathedral at Palma in Majorca and for the great parish church of Sta María del Mar at Barcelona (1329–83). At Gerona work began in 1312 at the east end under a mason named Enrique, but the notable design for the church as a whole, with its nave of a single span, belongs to Jacques Favran of Narbonne, who was in charge

87

88

90, 128

97

88 The Wiesen-
kirche of Soest in
Westphalia, built
between 1331 and
1376 to the design
of Johann
Schendeler. Its tall
windows and
moulded arches
without capitals
characterize one
type of fourteenth-
century German
church

from 1320 to 1347. The nave was not in fact built until after 1416, when an architectural conference had been held, attended by twelve masters from places as distant as Narbonne, Urgel, Tarragona and Tortosa. The old cathedral, La Seo, at Saragossa was rebuilt between 1316 and 1412, and important works were in progress at Valencia in 1330–60. But two of the most exquisite gems of small-scale design are the little cathedrals of Orihuela (1305–55), and Tortosa (1345–1441), begun by Benito Dalguayre.

89

In France it is evident that the architectural leadership of the West had been lost. The obvious reasons: civil discord due to the dynastic crisis of 1328 and later chronic war with England, cloak a deeper underlying cause of failure. Recent studies of Gothic structure by

90 At Gerona (*right*), the thirteenth-century scheme of the east end was given up when building was resumed in 1416, in favour of a wide nave embracing the whole width of chancel and aisles

89 *Above*: Puerta de las Cadenas at the small-scale cathedral of Orihuela, 1305–55

Dr Jacques Heyman have shown that the real life of French Gothic lasted only a century and a half, from the experiments leading to the new choir of Saint-Denis begun in 1140 to the collapse at Beauvais in 1284. Within that period the architectural style was not merely aesthetic, but the constant tentative expression of results achieved by trial-and-error in construction. The problems of weight, thrust, mass, wind-pressure, abutment and balance were continually mastered by the architects of the Île-de-France. In spite of the absence of any guiding mathematical theory (which indeed did not become effective before about 1800), the French masons were able to build up an empirical science which *did work*. The soundness of their methods was crowned by the successful fruit:

giant buildings which stood, and have continued to stand for many centuries unless wilfully destroyed.

After about the middle of the thirteenth century – say, after the death of St Louis in 1270 – this continuous experimentalism ceased, quenched by a phase of self-satisfaction. This reflected encyclopaedism in philosophy: the Schoolmen of the time had become satisfied that by now they knew all the answers, and thereafter might sit back happily. Such an attitude spells death, or stagnation, for any culture, and its counterpart among the building masters put an end to the main stream of Gothic impulse. Henceforward the separate national schools which had been offshoots from the French trunk became independent and, for another two centuries and more, pursued the experimental course. As we have seen, they received much from England, which was politically in the ascendant. France, too proud to accept aid from this quarter, even had it been forthcoming through the darkening veil of the Hundred Years War, almost ceased to build on the grand scale, and left several of its greatest buildings unfinished.

In spite of this, the story of French Gothic architecture was by no means done, and during the later fourteenth century a substantial amount of important work continued, especially for the King and the princes of the royal house. Notable for itself, and for its lasting impression upon the design of noble dwellings, was the old royal palace of the Louvre, begun in 1362 under Raymond du Temple, one of the greatest of French architects and founder of a dynasty. Throughout the century, and until the end of the Middle Ages, the most significant continuous centre of building activity was the

94 abbey of Saint-Ouen at Rouen, where the choir was built in 1319–39, perhaps to the design of Jean Camelin. Many details of Saint-Ouen served as pace-setters for the last two centuries of Gothic style, and show for how long the capital of Normandy retained its artistic vigour.

It may be said of the second half of the fourteenth century that it witnessed the climax of European art. The search of the artists for an underlying unity was rewarded, in the best works, with success. The sense of strain, so marked in earlier work, is no longer noted, and the greater buildings breathe a spirit of confidence and demonstrate the supremacy of achievement of which their authors were capable. Not only had individual buildings acquired artistic unity,

91 Venice produced its own version of Gothic – essentially a façade architecture of decorative carving and, in this case, polychrome brick

but every part and detail was so subtly proportioned to the whole, and to human scale, that it gives the impression of a work of nature rather than of human striving. A quality of glory – not secular pomp, nor elaboration of enrichment – informs the greatest architecture and the attendant carvings, paintings, embroideries and other minor arts which joined together as if in some orchestral symphony.

This quality, itself perhaps of Eastern inspiration, is marked in the buildings of Venice that so aroused the enthusiasm of John Ruskin. The work which could be carried out for the patrician patrons of a city-state unique in history, endowed with continuity of tradition, direct links with Byzantium and with the centres of world activity such as Cairo, and enormous wealth, enabled secular architecture to show to advantage. Elsewhere it is mainly in the churches that we must seek for the finest flights of Gothic enterprise; but in Venice it is the dwelling, the mansion, the palace that take the palm. The magnificent water front of the Doge's Palace was 91 begun in 1343 by Pietro Baseggio, and finished in 1404, thus spanning the period of two generations which marked the culmination of this refined yet rich, splendid and vigorous art.

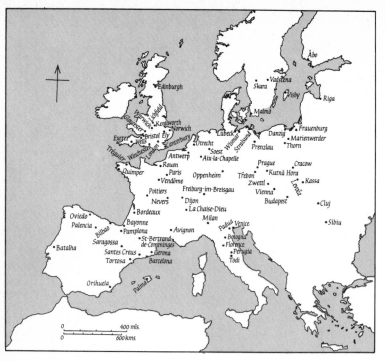

92 Chief architectural sites of the fourteenth century. By this time there was Gothic activity over the whole of Europe except for the Balkans and Russia, where the Eastern Orthodox Church maintained the Byzantine style

93 Architectural sites of the fifteenth century. The explosive energy of the earlier centuries shows little sign of slackening, in spite of political and economic recession

The abbey
church of Saint-
Ouen at Rouen,
one of the most
influential designs
of the later
Middle Ages,
was begun in
1319

The origin of the national English style, Perpendicular, has already been described; but something more must be said of the amazing outburst of art which accompanied the resurgence of England as a great European power. Unusual and even exotic themes, such as the octagon of Ely Cathedral, made their appearance during the first half of the century. There, the immense timber vault and lantern of 1328–40 were the work of William Hurley, one of the greatest of English carpenters, brought from London to design and supervise the works. Edward III completed and embellished the royal chapel of St Stephen at Westminster, and surrounded himself with architects and artists of the highest standing. Later in the century there came a second crop of noble works, largely the product of these royal artists or of their provincial pupils and associates. The grandiose state apartments of Kenilworth Castle, built for Edward's son John of Gaunt between 1372 and 1395, set a new trend in fashion, and the cathedrals and greater churches vied with one another to build and rebuild in the latest style. So at Canterbury the nave begun in 1379 was designed by the king's mason Henry Yevele, while that of Winchester, transformed for William of Wykeham from 1394, was the work of Yevele's colleague William Wynford, who had already designed Wykeham's two educational buildings, New College at Oxford and Winchester College, and was also architect to Wells Cathedral, where he designed the western towers. Yevele and the carpenter Hugh Herland renewed the great hall at Westminster in 1394–1400 where Herland's oak roof remains as the greatest single work of art of the whole of the European Middle Ages. No such combined achievement in the fields of mechanics and aesthetics remains elsewhere, nor is there any evidence for such a feat having ever existed. This amazing work owes its being to the taste and cultural energy of the King, Richard II, for whom the contemporary Wilton Diptych was painted, while Geoffrey Chaucer wrote his *Canterbury Tales*.

Though the new roof of Westminster Hall was the most remarkable work of its kind ever carried out, England had no monopoly of great halls, and had few civic buildings of notable size. Among the few worthy of mention is the London Guildhall, 153 feet long with a span of 49 feet, built in 1411–46 by the mason John Croxton. Comparison is interesting with Barcelona, another of the great

95 When the crossing tower of Ely collapsed in 1322 it was replaced by an unprecedented wooden octagon designed by the royal carpenter William Hurley

maritime capitals of western Europe, where the Hall of the Hundred was built between 1373 and 1402. Just as the London Guildhall was a reduced version of the king's hall at Westminster, so this municipal chamber at Barcelona was a reduction in scale of the King of Aragon's Tinell in the royal palace, built in 1359–70 by Guillem Carbonell. The kingdom of Aragon produced many noble public buildings, including Exchanges in Barcelona (1380–92), in Valencia (1483–98) and at Palma in the island of Majorca (1426–48), the last a distinguished design by Guillermo Sagrera, who had been architect of Perpignan Cathedral in 1416 and later moved to Naples, where from 1450 onwards he was rebuilding the Castel Nuovo. Barcelona still possesses another remarkable building in the Hospital of Santa Cruz, used until quite recently as a hospital but now the Central Library of Catalonia; its original buildings of 1401–15 remain structurally complete.

100

99

98

96, 97 The conjunction of royal palace and great church goes back to Carolingian times. At Westminster both palace and abbey date from before the Conquest. This plan shows them in the sixteenth century, the abbey church (a) surrounded by its monastic buildings (b), and the palace a rambling affair centred on the great hall (c, shown *right* with its magnificent hammer-beam roof, the work of Hugh Herland, 1394–1400). Other palace buildings include (d) St Stephen's Chapel, (e) the White Hall, and (f) the Jewel Tower

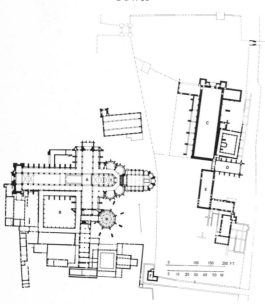

98–100 Outstanding civic buildings survive in Spain. *Top left:* the
former Hospital of Santa Cruz in Barcelona, 1401–15. *Lower left:* the
silk-exchange of Valencia, 1483–98. *Above:* the Tinell, the spacious hall
of the royal palace of Barcelona, built 1359–70 by Guillem Carbonell

101 The west front of
Beverley Minster, *c.* 1400,
is arguably the best of
English west fronts,
displaying all the force
and dignity inherent in
the Perpendicular style

The later fourteenth century and the first years of the fifteenth
century saw much activity on major building works. At all the
main centres of Europe the Gothic style was producing much of its
most distinguished output. In England the west front of Beverley
101 Minster (*c.* 1400) excelled almost everything previously done
23 at the cathedrals. In 1392 the great western tower of Ulm on the
Danube was started, though operations dragged on for just a
century before leaving the work unfinished until modern times.
As at Cologne and Strasbourg a succession of architects was responsible: Ulrich von Ensingen was the original designer, while the
upper stage of the tower, built in 1474–92, was the work of

102 St Stephen's, Vienna
– the steeple, begun in
1399, incorporated advice
from Peter Parler's son
Wenzel

Matthäus Böblinger, whose designs for the spire survived to permit *22*
ultimate completion. The steeple of St Stephen in Vienna, begun in *102*
1399, was built with advice from Wenzel Parler, son of the great
Peter, and completed in 1433 by Hans von Prachatitz, Peter Parler's
pupil.

In Portugal the period was enriched by the noble monastery of
Batalha, commemorating the battle in which independence was *66*
won. It was founded in 1387 and the first architect was Affonso
Domingues, who built most of the church and began the cloisters
before his death in 1402. Several features at Batalha are strongly
reminiscent of English Gothic, and there is no doubt that the alliance

between England and Portugal extended beyond the political field. In Spain the great undertaking of the fifteenth century was the *103, 104* construction of Seville Cathedral, the largest Gothic cathedral in *130* the world and planned deliberately to be 'so great and of such a kind that those who see it finished shall think we were mad', as one of the chapter said during consideration of the designs. The conclusion of the deliberations was expressed in a report that 'a new church shall be made so good that there shall be none its equal'. Seville is the great summation of Peninsular Gothic, borrowing ideas from

103, 104 'So great and of such a kind' was the cathedral of Seville to be 'that those who see it finished shall think we were mad.' Finished in 1506, it was among the last great cathedrals of Gothic Europe

Toledo, from Barcelona and from northern France. It seems probable that the architect was an expatriate Norman known in Spain as Carlín, but whose name was really Charles Gaultier, from Rouen. Likenesses of detail to the late fourteenth-century works in the Norman capital suggest that this must have been in fact the training-ground of the Seville designer.

Soon after the opening of the fifteenth century the political complexion of Europe changed for the worse. The Lancastrian usurpation of 1399 had set a bad tone in England, and was soon followed

in Bohemia by the Hussite wars of religion. France was to be ravaged by the renewed outbreak of the Hundred Years War. Though many great building works were in progress, some had to be suspended for long periods, as was the nave of Westminster Abbey; while Prague Cathedral was simply abandoned half-finished until the mid-nineteenth century. Some churches of considerable importance were built in outlying areas of Gothic Europe, as in northern Germany, Scandinavia and the Baltic region. In central and southern Germany several parish churches of very large scale belong to the middle of the century: St Georg in Dinkelsbühl, built in 1448–92 by Nicolaus Eseler; the choir of St Lorenz in Nuremberg (1445–72) by Konrad Roritzer; and the brick Frauenkirche in Munich (1468–88), designed by Jörg Ganghofer. In Hungary, St Elizabeth's Cathedral in Kassa belongs to the hundred years 1380–1480, while St Maurice at Olomouc (Olmütz) in Moravia is a hall-church spanning the years 1412–91.

105

105 The Frauenkirche at Munich, 1468–88, a brick cathedral in a country lacking stone

106 The richly ornate Chapel of the Constable was added to Burgos Cathedral in 1482–94 by the son of 'Juan de Colonia', Simón, now completely hispanicized

The rekindling fire

Towards the end of the century, however, a new breath of energy swept across the scene. The embers of Gothic art were rekindled into a final blaze of glory which enriched every European country apart from the determinedly classical Italy. It would be impossible even to enumerate within a small compass the major churches alone, and only a selection of the most outstanding works can be mentioned. Between about 1480 and 1550 or even later, many of the most truly magnificent buildings of all time were erected, in England, in Flanders and the Netherlands, in Germany, Bohemia and Poland, and in Spain and Portugal. And while these greater monuments of church art were in progress, it must not be overlooked that castles, palaces, mansions, universities, colleges, guildhalls and other public and private secular buildings also formed part of the great and rich harvest.

At this time the dominance had passed to Flanders, or at least to the powerful Dukes of Burgundy who held sway over a great area of eastern France, geographically speaking, as well as over the whole of modern Belgium, Holland and Luxembourg, together with adjacent parts of north-eastern France. Within their dominions a rich style, based on that of late fourteenth-century France, but

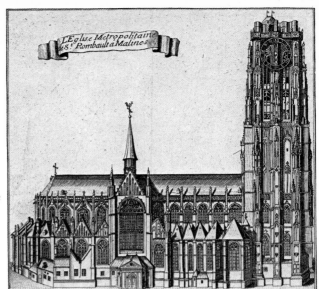

107, 108 In Flanders the most ambitious buildings belong to the later Middle Ages. The cathedral of St Bavon at Ghent (*left*) was begun in 1274 but the tower was not complete until 1533. At Malines (*right*) the vast tower was never finished

more opulent and at times overburdened with enrichment, came into being. At the giant cathedral of Antwerp, which had been started in 1352, the west front was built in 1422–74, and then the enormous tower of Rombaut Keldermans and Dominique de Waghemakere, finished in 1518. At Ghent the nave and tower of St Bavon were built between 1461 and 1533, while at Malines the outstanding feature is the vast but never quite finished tower begun in 1452 by Andries Keldermans, and continued by his son Antoon. In Holland the main influence came from Utrecht Cathedral whose tower of 1321–82 by Jan van Henegouwen was the model for several others, among them that of Breda (1468–1509). The great Dutch church of the end of the Middle Ages was the cathedral at 's Hertogenbosch, where the choir had been built in 1419–39. But the nave and the famous sculptures belong to the period 1478–1529, mainly under the direction of Alard van Hameel.

107
108

Flemish masters travelled to Spain and to England, and much of the vivid panash of late Gothic is undoubtedly due to them. They were not the only migrant influences, however, for as we have seen the western steeples at Burgos are due to a German mason from Cologne, and the later works completing the cathedral were designed by his son Simón and grandson Francisco de Colonia. Simón de Colonia built the chapel of Sta Ana (1477–82) and the

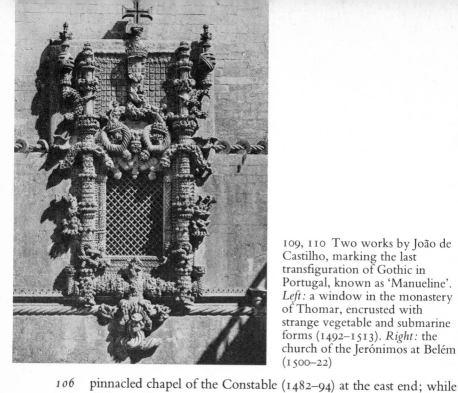

109, 110 Two works by João de
Castilho, marking the last
transfiguration of Gothic in
Portugal, known as 'Manueline'.
Left: a window in the monastery
of Thomar, encrusted with
strange vegetable and submarine
forms (1492–1513). *Right:* the
church of the Jerónimos at Belém
(1500–22)

106   pinnacled chapel of the Constable (1482–94) at the east end; while
the central lantern, completing the composition of the whole building, was put up in 1540–68 under his son Francisco. Elsewhere in
Spain the same architects were at work: Simón de Colonia began
the cathedral at Astorga in 1471, to be continued between 1530 and
1559 by Rodrigo Gil de Hontañón. At Plasencia a vast new cathedral
was started in 1498 by Enrique de Egas, to be continued under
Francisco de Colonia and Juan de Álava in 1513–37. But the two
greatest works of the last Gothic age in Spain were the new
cathedrals of Salamanca, begun in 1512, and Segovia (1522), both
by Juan Gil de Hontañón and continued by his son Rodrigo. In
109   Portugal the two grand works were the convent of Thomar (1492–
1513) by João de Castilho, who also completed the Jeronimos at
110   Belém, begun in 1500. Possibly even more remarkable, as an
example of the strange sculptural style named after King Manuel I
(1495–1521), are the unfinished chapels at the east end of Batalha,
begun in 1503–09 by Matheus Fernandes, one of the greatest
examples of invention in architecture and a glory not only of
Portugal but of Europe.

118

111 In such works as the Vladislav Hall at Prague (1493–1503), by Benedikt Ried, Gothic rib-vaults have become a purely decorative pattern of intertwining lines

Architects of outstanding genius sprang up in all quarters. In
113 Moravia the magnificent church of St James at Brno (Brünn), in course of construction from 1480 to 1552, owes most to Anton Pilgram, master from 1495 to 1515; while in Bohemia an extra-ordinary style of rococo Gothic, with curving vault-ribs and spacious vistas, was created by Benedikt Ried. Ried, author of the
111 Vladislav Hall in Prague Castle (1493–1503) and the nave of St
112 Barbara at Kutná Hora (*c.* 1540), may be considered the last Gothic genius of central Europe. Meanwhile there had been an Indian summer of Gothic art throughout the whole of the Baltic region and a Polish *flamboyant* style appears in the church of St Anne at Vilna (1516), and in the Jagellonian Library (1492–97) at Cracow, with cellular ribless vaults, found earlier in eastern Spain, and in this period also in Bohemia.

112 The vaults of St Barbara, Kutná Hora – that of the choir (*centre*),
c. 1400 by Peter Parler; that of the nave (*top*) by Benedikt Ried, *c.* 1540

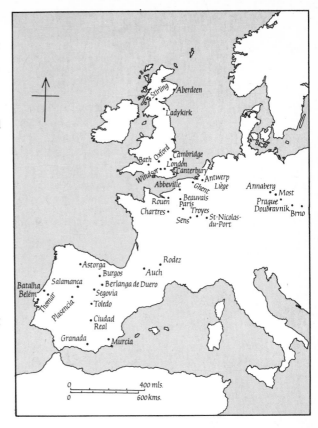

113 *Left:* the church of St James at Brno, begun in 1480, but completed after 1495 by Anton Pilgram, one of the architects who created a final flowering of Gothic in Bohemia and Moravia

114 Chief architectural sites of the sixteenth century. The retreat of Gothic to the north and west before the withering blast of the Renaissance can be clearly seen; but the intense vitality of Gothic is still marked, since this map represents the activity of only fifty, not of a hundred years

Returning to France, where the *flamboyant* style and enriched detail had at last taken root, we find notable architects once more at work. Several cathedrals were adding new fronts in the latest style, and the last of the great cathedral churches was begun at Auch 116 by Jean Chesneau in 1489. Saint-Wulfran at Abbeville (1488–1539), Saint-Nicolas-du-Port in Lorraine (1494–1530) by Simon Moyset, 115 and the church of Saint-Jacques-de-la-Boucherie in Paris, of which the noble tower survives (1509–23), by Jean de Felin, must stand for the greater churches. Secular building is exemplified by the Palais de Justice of Rouen, designed by Roger Ango and Roulland le Roux (1499–1526). Le Roux also designed the central west front of Rouen Cathedral (1509–14), while his greatest rival, Martin 117 Chambiges of Paris, was responsible for transeptal fronts at Sens (1494), Beauvais (1499) and the main front of Troyes (1502–31). It 118

123

may have been Chambiges who inspired the last daydream of French Gothic: an immense steeple rising to 502 feet in height, over the crossing of Beauvais. The work was done by Jean Vast, son of an elder Jean Vast who worked under Chambiges; the spire was finished in 1569, but collapsed four years later. Vast lived to complete the necessary repairs to the church below, but the steeple was never rebuilt. The fire of Gothic aspiration had at last died down.

115, 116 Two of the last great French Gothic churches – Saint-Nicolas-du-Port (1494–1530) by Simon Moyset, and the cathedral of Auch, begun in 1489 by Jean Chesneau

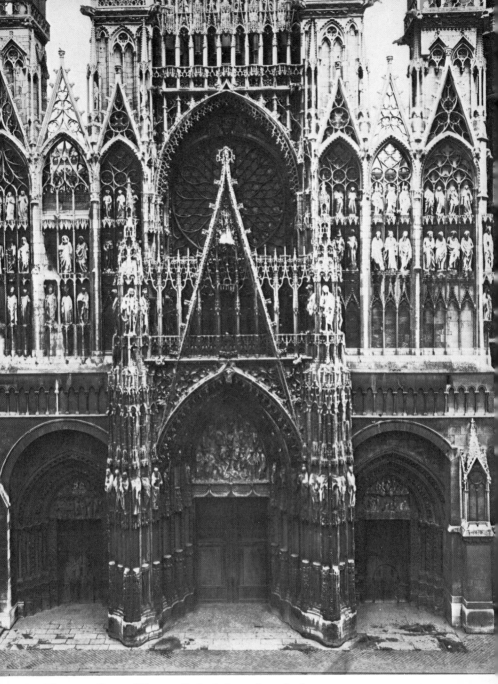

117 The west front of Rouen Cathedral consists of a lacy stone screen
designed by Roulland le Roux in 1509 to cover the earlier façade

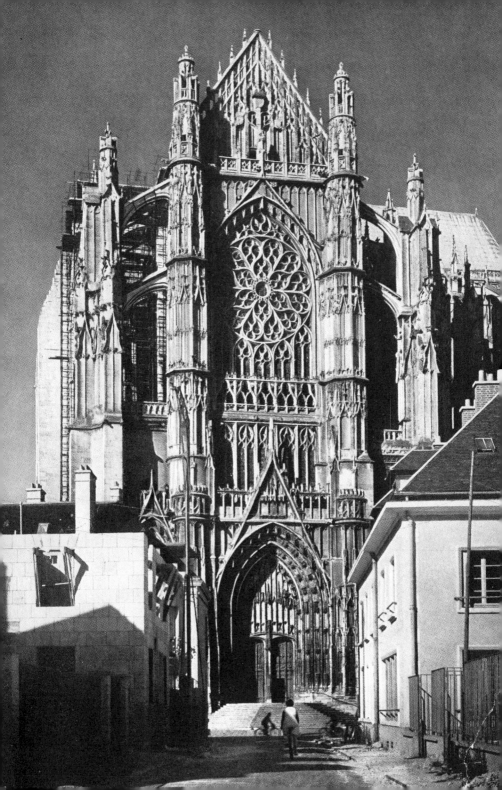

118 Beauvais, the highest cathedral in Christendom, was never carried further than the crossing. In 1499–1549 it was given its superb south transept front (*left*) by Martin Chambiges of Paris

119 At Canterbury, Henry Yevele's nave was crowned between 1493 and 1505 by the noble crossing tower known as 'Bell Harry' (*right*) designed by John Wastell

For a final glimpse of the style whose elements first appeared together at Durham about 1100, we return to England. The 'white robe of churches' of an earlier period was renewed once more in the terrific outburst of architectural exuberance which swept the country between the return from exile of Edward IV in 1471, and the dissolution of the last monasteries by Henry VIII in 1540. Among the host of masons and carpenters employed, a few stand out as men of profound genius. Such were John Wastell, designer of the great Bell Harry tower of Canterbury Cathedral (1493–1505) and of the eastern chapels of Peterborough Cathedral, under whom the magnificent chapel of King's College at Cambridge was completed (1508–15). The brothers Robert and William Vertue were

119

120, 121 The last invention of English Gothic was the pendent vault, exemplified in Henry VII's Chapel, Westminster, the way by which it seems to defy the laws of gravity is explained in the diagram

120, 121 the king's chief masons to Henry VII and Henry VIII, and jointly designed the new Bath Abbey of 1501–39, and Henry VII's Chapel at Westminster (1503–19). William Vertue also designed Corpus Christi College, Oxford (1512–18) and completed St George's Chapel at Windsor, of which he designed the west front (c. 1500–27). Along with William Vertue, who died in 1527, and his colleague Henry Redman, one of Cardinal Wolsey's architects, there worked the great carpenter Humphrey Coke, whose roof over the hall of Christ Church, Oxford, is the last triumph of English Gothic carpentry.

Gothic had had its day: its complex systems of proportion made no appeal to the dilettanti of a new age, intoxicated with notions of Roman grandeur and suffering from an overdose of simplified Vitruvius. The will-of-the-wisp of spurious antiquity lured wealthy patrons away from those architects still learned in tradition, and

128

substituted foreign pattern-books for the parchment skins and plaster tracing-floors which had displayed the living art of five hundred years. Religious fanaticism and material self-interest concluded an unholy alliance to destroy the outmoded art, and the great buildings became too often mere stone quarries from which pillaged materials might be drawn. Yet in spite of the enormous scale of destruction, starting in the middle of the sixteenth century and continuing for four hundred years until the present time, enough of the Gothic stones is left to bear witness. In sheer bulk of material shifted, in area covered, in space enveloped, it is evident that the Gothic age was pre-eminent among all the cultural epochs known, through recorded history and about the globe. This was the outcome of profound religious inspiration, however misguided it may sometimes have been. It is hard to justify the Crusades as an expression of the Christian spirit; but we must accept that among their consequences was the origin of the greatest art the world has yet seen. And in remembering the crusaders we may think also of their corps of engineers, recruited from among the most skilled artists and craftsmen then to be found in the West: sharing the danger and heat of the day, but still finding time and energy to make note of beautiful details or strange skills. To those that came back, bearing this harvest with them, we owe the greater and enduring harvest of the glorious world of Gothic art.

122 The builders of Chartres. This drawing from a stained-glass window shows a master-mason checking a wall with a plumb-line and stone-cutters shaping stones. In the arches hang templates for mouldings, a plan, compasses and level

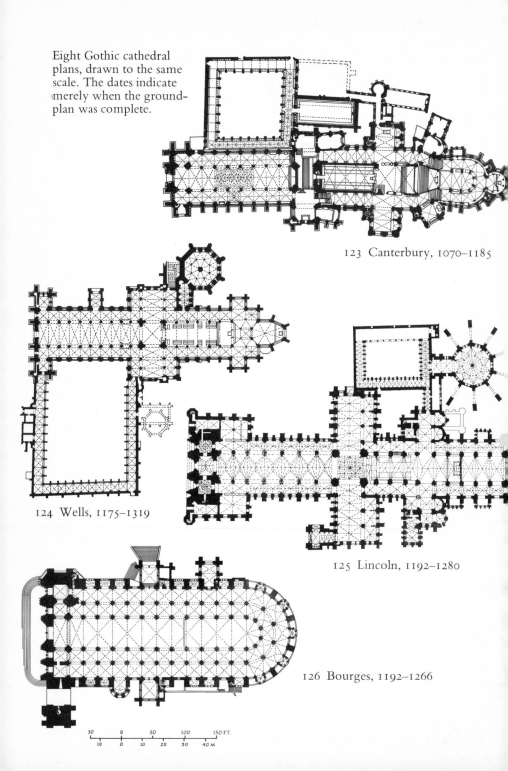

Eight Gothic cathedral plans, drawn to the same scale. The dates indicate merely when the ground-plan was complete.

123 Canterbury, 1070–1185

124 Wells, 1175–1319

125 Lincoln, 1192–1280

126 Bourges, 1192–1266

50   0   50   100   150 FT.
10   0   10   20   30   40 M

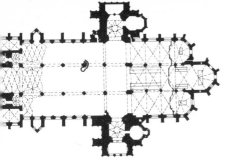

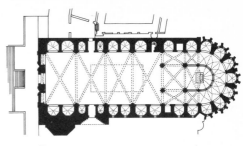

128 Gerona, 1312–1420

27 Vienna, 1304–1440

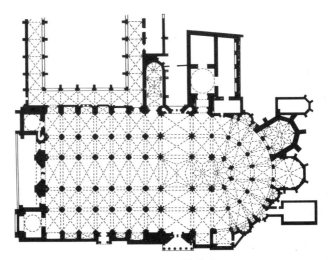

129 Toledo, 1226–1400

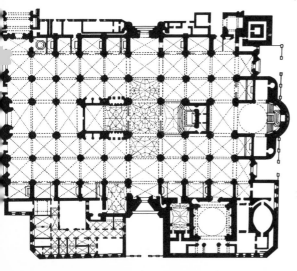

130 Seville, 1400–1498

Select Bibliography

The appended list of books includes titles chosen for three main reasons: to provide references; to give additional illustrations; and to offer further reading in which various topics may be followed. Contributions to periodicals have not been included, but a few which contain matter not yet published elsewhere must be mentioned:

ROBERT BRANNER, 'Drawings from a Thirteenth-century Architect's Shop: the Reims Palimpsest', in *Journal of the Society of Architectural Historians* (Philadelphia), XVII, 1958; 'Villard de Honnecourt, Reims, and the Origin of Gothic Architectural Drawing', in *Gazette des Beaux-Arts* (Paris), March 1963; FRANÇOIS BUCHER, 'Design in Gothic Architecture – a Preliminary Assessment', in *Journal of the Society of Architectural Historians*, XXVII, 1968; KENNETH HARRISON, 'Vitruvius and Acoustic Jars in England during the Middle Ages', in *Transactions of the Ancient Monuments Society* (London), New Series XV, 1968; JOHN H. HARVEY, 'Winchester College', in *Journal of the British Archaeological Association*, 3rd Series, XXVIII, 1965; 'The Origins of Gothic Architecture: Some Further Thoughts', in *The Antiquaries Journal*, XLVIII, 1968; 'The Tracing Floor in York Minster', in *Report of the Friends of York Minster*, XL for 1968, 1969; JACQUES HEYMAN, 'The Stone Skeleton', in *International Journal of Solids Structures*, II, 1966; 'Beauvais Cathedral', in *Transactions of the Newcomen Society*, XL for 1967–68; 'On the Rubber Vaults of the Middle Ages, and other matters', in *Gazette des Beaux-Arts*, March 1968; L. R. SHELBY, 'Mediaeval Masons' Tools: Compass and Square', in *Technology and Culture* (Chicago), VI, 1965.

AUBERT, M. *L'Architecture cistercienne en France*, 2nd ed., 2 vols. (Paris, 1947)
AUBERT, M., SCHMOLL, J. A. and HOFSTÄTTER, H. H. *Le gothique à son apogée* (Paris, 1964); English trs. *High Gothic Art* (London, 1964)

◀ 131 A French manuscript of 1448 gives a picture of building methods in the Middle Ages. Of the church in the foreground, the chancel has been completed and work is proceeding on the nave – a brick core, with stone facing, and darker stone for the mouldings of doors and windows. The other churches are nearly complete, the spires having been left till last

BOASE, T. S. R. *English Art 1100–1216* (Oxford, 1953)

BOCK, H. *Der Decorated Style* (Heidelberger Kunstgeschichtliche Abhandlungen, Neue Folge, Band 6, Heidelberg, 1962)

BOND, F. *Gothic Architecture in England* (London, 1906)
An Introduction to English Church Architecture, 2 vols. (London, 1913)

BRANNER, R. *St. Louis and the Court Style in Gothic Architecture* (London, 1965)

BRIEGER, P. H. *English Art 1216–1307* (Oxford, 1957)

BRIGGS, M. S. *The Architect in History* (Oxford, 1927)

BROOKE, C. *The Twelfth Century Renaissance* (London, 1969)

BROWN, R. A. *English Medieval Castles* (London, 1954; revised ed. *English Castles*, London, 1962)

CAMÓN, J. *Simón García: Compendio de arquitectura y simetría de los templos* (Madrid, 1941)

CLAPHAM, A. W. *Romanesque Architecture in Western Europe* (Oxford, 1936)

COLOMBIER, P. DU *Les Chantiers des cathédrales* (Paris, 1953)

CONANT, K. J. *Carolingian and Romanesque Architecture 800 to 1200*, 2nd ed. (Harmondsworth, 1966)
Cluny – Les Eglises et la Maison du Chef d'Ordre (Mâcon, 1968)

COULTON, G. G. *Art and the Reformation* (Oxford, 1928)

COX, G. T. *Jehan Foucquet, native of Tours* (London, 1931)

CRESWELL, K. A. C. *The Muslim Architecture of Egypt*, 2 vols. (Oxford, 1952–60)
A Short Account of Early Muslim Architecture (Harmondsworth, 1958)

ESCHAPASSE, M. *L'architecture bénédictine en Europe* (Paris, 1963)

EVANS, JOAN *Art in Mediaeval France 987–1498* (London, 1948)
English Art 1307–1461 (Oxford, 1949)

FOCILLON, H. *Art d'Occident: le moyen âge roman et gothique* (Paris, 1938); English trs. *The Art of the West in the Middle Ages*, 2 vols. (London, 1963)

FRANKL, P. *The Gothic: Literary Sources and Interpretations through Eight Centuries* (Princeton, 1960)

GRIMSCHITZ, B. *Hanns Puchspaum* (Vienna, 1947)

GRIVOT, D. and ZARNECKI, G. *Gislebertus, Sculptor of Autun* (London, 1961)

HAHNLOSER, H. R. *Villard de Honnecourt* (Vienna, 1935)

HARVEY, J. H. *Henry Yevele, c. 1320 to 1400. The life of an English architect* 2nd ed. (London, 1946)
Gothic England. A Survey of national culture, 1300–1550, 2nd ed. (London, 1948)
The Gothic World, 1100–1600. A survey of architecture and art (London, 1950; paperback New York, 1969)
English Mediaeval Architects. A biographical dictionary down to 1550 (London, 1954)
The Cathedrals of Spain (London, 1957)
English Cathedrals, revised paperback ed. (London, 1963)

HASKINS, C. H. *Studies in the History of Mediaeval Science*, 2nd ed. (Cambridge, Mass., 1927)

HAYTER, W. *William of Wykeham, Patron of the Arts* (London, 1970)

JOPE, E. M. (ed.) *Studies in Building History* (London, 1961)

KLETZL, O. *Plan-Fragmente aus der deutschen Dombauhütte von Prag* (Stuttgart, 1939)

KNOOP, D. and JONES, G. P. *The Mediaeval Mason*, 3rd ed. (Manchester, 1967)

LAMPÉREZ Y ROMEA, V. *Historia de la Arquitectura Cristiana Española en la Edad Media*, 2nd ed., 3 vols. (Madrid, 1930)
Arquitectura Civil Española, 2 vols. (Madrid, 1922)

LASTEYRIE DU SAILLANT, R. DE *L'Architecture religieuse en France à l'époque gothique*, ed. M. Aubert, 2 vols. (Paris, 1926)
L'Architecture religieuse en France à l'époque romane, 2nd ed. (Paris, 1929)

LETHABY, W. R. *Mediaeval Art from the Peace of the Church to the Eve of the Renaissance 312–1350* (London, 1904)
Westminster Abbey and the Kings' Craftsmen (London, 1906)
Westminster Abbey Re-examined (London, 1925)

MORGAN, B. G. *Canonic Design in English Mediaeval Architecture* (Liverpool, 1961)

MORTET, V. and DESCHAMPS, P. *Recueil de textes relatifs à l'histoire de l'architecture et à la condition des architectes en France, au moyen âge, XIe–XIIIe siècles*, 2 vols. (Paris, 1911–29)

PANOFSKY, E. *Abbot Suger on the Abbey Church of St.-Denis and its Art Treasures* (Princeton, 1946)

RICKMAN, T. and PARKER, J. H. *Gothic Architecture*, 7th ed. (Oxford, 1881)

SALZMAN, L. F. *Building in England down to 1540. A documentary history*, revised ed. (Oxford, 1967)

SCHELLER, R. W. *A Survey of Medieval Model Books* (Haarlem, 1963)

STEIN, H. *Les Architectes des cathédrales gothiques* (Paris, 1909)

STEWART, C. *Early Christian, Byzantine, and Romanesque Architecture* (Simpson's History of Architectural Development, new ed., vol. II, London, 1954)
Gothic Architecture (ibid., vol. III, London, 1961)

STREET, G. E. *Some Account of Gothic Architecture in Spain*, 2nd ed. (London, 1869)

SWARTWOUT, R. E. *The Monastic Craftsman* (Cambridge, 1932)

TURNER, T. H. and PARKER, J. H. *Some Account of Domestic Architecture in England*, 3 vols. in 4 (Oxford, 1851–59)

WILLIS, R. *The Architectural History of Canterbury Cathedral* (London, 1845)

WILLIS, R. and CLARK, J. W. *The Architectural History of the University of Cambridge and of the Colleges of Cambridge and Eton*, 4 vols. (Cambridge, 1886)

WOOD, MARGARET *The English Mediaeval House* (London, 1965)

List of Illustrations

east from the north transept; 1255-77, perhaps begun by Enrique de Burgos, continued by Juan Pérez. Photo Mas

58 Salisbury: exterior of the Cathedral from the south-east; by Nicholas of Ely, c. 1220-60, tower by Richard of Farleigh, begun 1334. Photo Edwin Smith

59 Wells: west front of the Cathedral; lower part by Thomas Norreys, 1220-60, towers designed after 1365 by William Wynford. Photo A.F. Kersting

60 Durham: interior of the eastern transept of the Cathedral, The Chapel of the Nine Altars; by Richard Farnham, begun 1242. Photo Courtauld Institute of Art

61 Map showing the chief architectural sites of western Europe in the thirteenth century. Drawing by John Woodcock

62 Narbonne: section through the choir of the Cathedral; begun 1272. Drawing by Martin Weaver after H. Nodet

63 Rheims: detail of west front; designed by Bernard de Soissons, built c. 1255-90. Photo Martin Hürlimann

64 Bristol: plan of the north porch of St Mary Redcliffe; first quarter of the fourteenth century. Drawing by John Stengelhofen

65 Bristol: north doorway of the north porch of St Mary Redcliffe; first quarter of the fourteenth century. Drawing by John Stengelhofen

66 Batalha: bay in the Royal Cloister of the abbey; begun 1387, tracery c. 1500-10. Photo Courtauld Institute of Art

67 Lincoln: The 'Bishop's Eye' in the south transept of the Cathedral; c. 1330. Photo National Monuments Record

68 Amiens: rose window (surrounded by a wheel of fortune) in the south transept front of the Cathedral; c. 1500. Photo Jeiter

69 Cairo: detail of mihrab (prayer-niche) wall in the tomb of Mustafa Pasha; 1269-73. Drawing by Ian Mackenzie Kerr after Creswell, *The Muslim Architecture of Egypt*, Vol. II

70 Norwich: tracery in two bays of the south walk of the Cathedral cloister; by William Ramsey, c. 1324. Drawing by John Harvey

71 Ely: detail of a bay in the Cathedral choir; 1320s. Drawing by John Harvey

72 Ely: detail of wall of the Cathedral Lady Chapel; c. 1335-39. Drawing by John Harvey

73 London: tracery in a bay of the cloister of Old St Paul's; begun by William Ramsay, 1332. Drawing by John Harvey after archaeological evidence and an engraving by Wenceslaus Hollar

74 Wells: east window of the Cathedral; c. 1339. Drawing by John Harvey

75 Gloucester: south transept window of the Cathedral; c. 1335. Drawing by Martin Weaver

76 Gloucester: east window of the Cathedral; c. 1351. Drawing by Martin Weaver

77 Norwich: bay in the south walk of the Cathedral cloister; by William Ramsey, c. 1324. Photo Jarrolds

78 Santes Creus: the abbey cloister; 1332-36 and 1347-51. Photo Mas

79 Santes Creus: detail of a capital in the abbey cloister; probably 1347-51. Photo courtesy of the estate of the late Don José Vives i Miret

80 Santes Creus: tracery in the bays of the abbey cloisters; by Reinard des Fonoll, 1332-36 and 1347-51. Photo courtesy of the estate of the late Don José Vives i Miret

81 Bristol: section through the Cathedral choir, with the Berkeley Chapel on the right; c. 1311-40. Drawing by Martin Weaver

82 Bristol: vault of the south choir aisle in the Cathedral; c. 1311-40. Photo Reece Winston

83 Bristol: skeleton vault of the Berkeley Chapel vestibule in the Cathedral; c. 1311-40. Photo National Monuments Record

84 Gloucester: interior of the Cathedral cloister; from c. 1370. Photo Edwin Smith

85 Prague: section through the Cathedral choir (north half); begun by Mathieu d'Arras, 1344-52, continued by Peter Parler. Drawing by R.C. Donovan

86 Prague: interior of the Cathedral choir; begun by Mathieu d'Arras, 1344-52, continued by Peter Parler. Photo Státní Ústav Památkcove Péče a Ochrany Přírody v Praze

87 Freiburg-im-Breisgau: interior of the

139

Index

140